"WITH THE TWENTY-SECOND"

Some of the Twenty-second Awaiting Relief at Ville-sur-Ancre.
Sketched at night in the "Big Caterpillar" by Lieut. Will Dyson.

"With The Twenty-Second"

A History of the Twenty-Second Battalion, A.I.F.

By

Captain E. GORMAN, M.C.

With an Introduction by
General Sir W. R. BIRDWOOD
G.C.M.G., K.C.B., K.C.S.I., C.I.E., D.S.O., A.D.C.

Frontispiece by
Lieut. WILL DYSON

The Naval & Military Press Ltd

Published by
The Naval & Military Press Ltd
5 Riverside, Brambleside, Bellbrook
Industrial Estate, Uckfield, East Sussex,
TN22 1QQ England
Tel: +44 (0) 1825 749494
Fax: +44 (0) 1825 765701
www.naval-military-press.com
www.military-genealogy.com
www.militarymaproom.com

In reprinting in facsimile from the original, any imperfections are inevitably reproduced and the quality may fall short of modern type and cartographic standards.

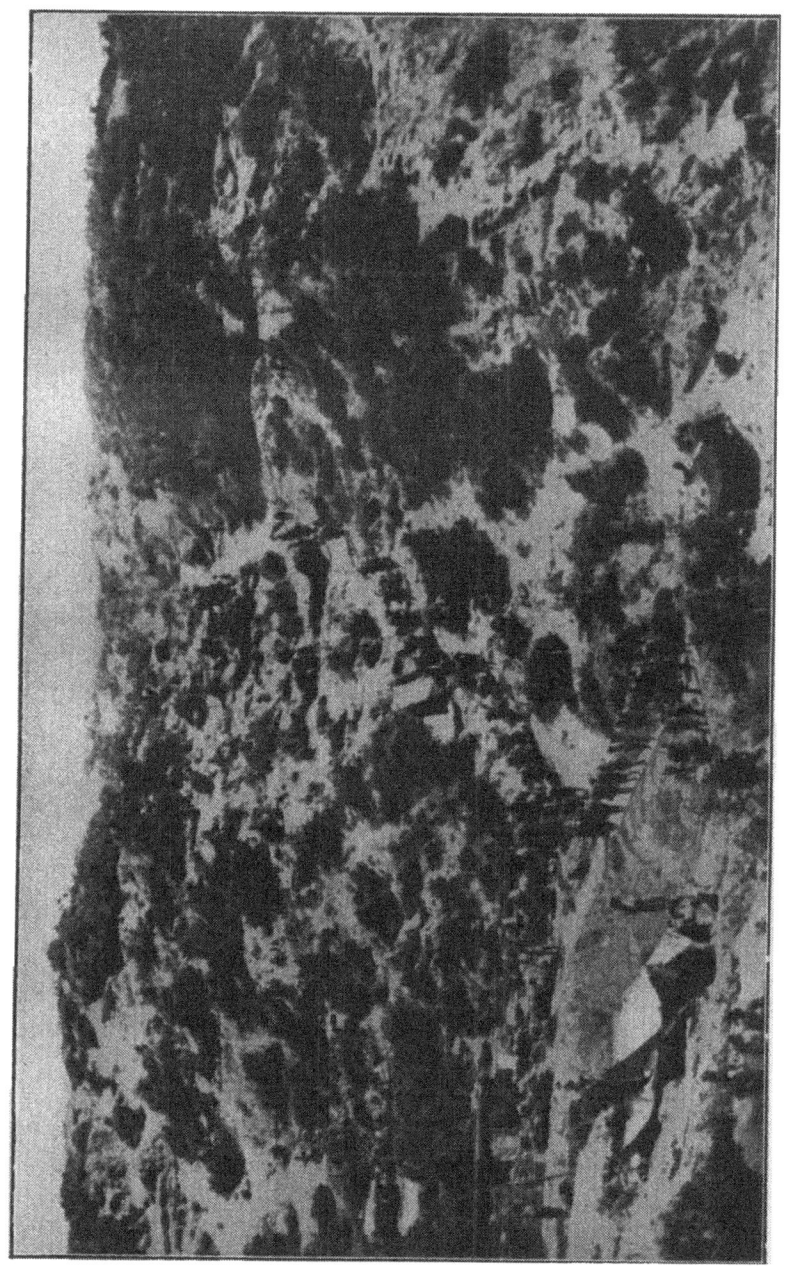

Battalion moving into Gallipoli trenches.

To the
Men who Died
this Book is
Dedicated

INTRODUCTION

By

General Sir W. R. BIRDWOOD, G.C.M.G., K.C.B., K.C.S.I., C.I.E., D.S.O., A.D.C.

I AM very pleased to have this opportunity of writing a short Introduction to "The History of the 22nd Battalion."

This history will, I am sure, be much appreciated as an intimate and interesting record contributed by members of a Battalion which has so fully played its part in building up and maintaining the magnificent reputation of the Australian Imperial Force, from the day it received its baptism of fire on the Gallipoli Peninsula to its final operation at Beaurevoir, immediately preceding the final collapse of the enemy.

It has been my great privilege to have served with the A.I.F. from the days of its infancy, and during its growth through years of stress and hardship, to the highly efficient force it now is. It is only natural that my feelings for the Australian soldier should have developed into a deep affection, while I am and shall always be proud to think that I am one in that large circle of comradeship which is so strongly evidenced in our Force. It is a friendship that cannot be too highly valued, and has been no small factor in the career of the A.I.F.; for I think I can safely say that this admirable trait so strongly developed in the character of our men of "sticking to a comrade" has been a propelling force, not only in many individual deeds of bravery and self-sacrifice, but in carrying through many a hard-fought engagement to success.

The Great War has called for all the finest qualities with which man is endowed, and which have been manifested so strongly in the Australian soldier. His tenacity of purpose, his resource and initiative, have been no less conspicuous than his indomitable valour; and these, combined with an inherent and ardent patriotism and love of country, have produced in him a soldier who has gained not only the full respect of the enemy as an adversary to be feared, but the admiration of all who have fought alongside him as comrades.

INTRODUCTION

No one will gainsay the intense patriotism of the Australian soldier. He is perhaps primarily an Australian, and a lover of all things Australian. This spirit may be said to dominate his thoughts and actions. But it is also the foundation of an equally strong and wider Imperial sentiment, which has been demonstrated with telling effect by the manhood of Australia and the other Dominions, who so spontaneously rallied to the Old Flag in defence of the principles of Justice and Liberty.

Australia may confidently rely on such men to fulfil faithfully and loyally the responsible duties of citizenship, and to maintain her traditions and honour, which her Forces have so firmly established on the battlefield.

W. R. Birdwood

29th January, 1919.

PREFACE

IT was during the German offensive of 1918, at a time when the end of the war seemed very remote, that the idea was formed of publishing, while the Unit was still abroad, this modest souvenir "History" of a famous Australian Battalion. The cessation of hostilities, however, caused its publication to be postponed until the Battalion's return to Australia.

Most of the book was written on the Somme at irregular intervals, in dugouts or ruined villages, or beneath that well-known tarpaulin which, in the forward area, served as Quartermaster's Store. The concluding chapters were written in Belgium.

Its sole aim is to offer an acceptable memento to the thousands who have passed through the Battalion, and to the relatives of our gallant fallen comrades. It is for relatives in particular that the book has been written, and, in their interests, there has been no striving after literary effect, but, instead, a detailed attention to dates and names of places, so that they may be able to identify more easily the period in which they are most interested.

It is a plain, unvarnished tale of the Battalion's deeds and wanderings during the four years of war. For the material of the earlier chapters I am indebted to those officers and men who so kindly lent their diaries, and, above all, to Lieutenant-Colonel A. R. L. Wiltshire, C.M.G., D.S.O., M.C., and Captain D. T. Miles

To the Battalion's Commanding Officer, Colonel Wiltshire, the book owes its origin. Without his supervision and sustained interest its publication would not have been achieved.

To General Sir W. R. Birdwood, G.C.M.G., K.C.B., K.C.S.I., C.I.E., D.S.O., A.D.C., for his Foreword, and to Lieutenant Will Dyson for his Frontispiece, I am greatly indebted.

The photographs of the various Companies were taken by the Official Photographer, Captain G. Wilkins, M.C., and his staff, in May and June, 1918, at Franvillers and Querrieu, on the Somme, and permission to use these photographs has kindly been given by the A.I.F. Publications Department.

EUGENE GORMAN.

"Any profits accruing from the sale of this book will be devoted to the funds of the 22nd Battalion Association."

Most of the photographs in this book were taken by the Official Photographer. Permission to reproduce them has kindly been given by the A.I.F. Publication Section, 130 Horseferry Road, London.

CONTENTS

	Page
Introduction	5
Preface	7

Chapter.
I.	Early Days, March-June, 1915	9
II.	Egypt, June-August, 1915	14
III.	Gallipoli, September-December, 1915	18
IV.	Mudros-Marseilles, December, 1915-March, 1916	24
V.	The First Months in France, March-July, 1916	28
VI.	Pozieres, July-August, 1916	33
VII.	Mouquet Farm, August, 1916	39
VIII.	Ypres, September-October, 1916	42
IX.	Winter on the Somme, November, 1916-January, 1917	44
X.	The German Withdrawal, February-April, 1917	48
XI.	Bullecourt, May, 1917	53
XII.	Bullecourt to Broodseinde, May-September, 1917	58
XIII.	Ypres, September-November, 1917	63
XIV.	Winter, November, 1917-March, 1918	70
XV.	The Somme Once More, April-May, 1918	75
XVI.	Ville-sur-Ancre, May, 1918	80
XVII.	To Villers-Bretonneux, May-August, 1918	84
XVIII.	Villers-Bretonneux and Herleville, August, 1918	88
XIX.	Cappy and Mont St. Quentin, August-September, 1918	94
XX.	Beaurevoir-Mont Brehain, October, 1918	99
XXI.	October, 1918-May, 1919	103

Appendix.
I.	Transport at Salonika	107
II.	Total Casualties	109
III.	Decorations	110
Roll of Honour		117

LIST OF ILLUSTRATIONS

Frontispiece	To face page 3
Battalion Moving into Gallipoli Trenches	4
Lieutenant-Colonel R. A. Crouch V.D.	12
Lieutenant-Colonel (later Brig.-General) R. Smith, C.M.G., D.S.O.	16
Sniper and Observer at Gallipoli	20
A Boxing Match at Hog's Back	28
O.G.1. Pozieres	32
Mouquet Farm	36
Zonnebeke, J.O.T., 4th October, 1917	41
Aeroplane Photo. of Beaurevoir Battlefield	42
Lieut-Colonel A. R. L. Wiltshire, C.M.G., D.S.O., M.C.	44
Chaplain-Captain F. H. Durnford, M.C.	48
Bullecourt Battlefield	52
A Little Game	56
Officers, June, 1918	57
Cookers at Martinpuich	60
Near Bellevarde Wood	64
Some of the Boys at Westhoek	65
Some Ville-sur-Ancre Trophies	80
Some Old Originals	81
Lieutenant W Ruthven, V.C.	84
Some Well-Known Characters	88
Officers, September, 1917	89
Le Sars	92
Kit and Kat, Westhoek	96
Hyde Park Corner, Ploegsteert	101
Pillbox Occupied by Battalion Headquarters, near Hannebeke	109

Battalion Headquarters' Company, June, 1918.
"A" Company, June, 1918.
"B" Company, June, 1918.
"C" Company, June, 1918.
"D" Company, June, 1918.
Transport Section, June, 1918.
Part of Nucleus Company, June, 1918.
Part of Nucleus Company, June, 1918.

"With The Twenty-Second"

CHAPTER I.

EARLY DAYS—MARCH-JUNE, 1915.

Although many of the original members of the 22nd Battalion, A.I.F., went into Broadmeadows Camp during the concluding months of 1914, it was not until 26th March, 1915, that they were drafted from the Depot. On that date the Battalion was officially formed, and Lieut.-Colonel R. A. Crouch, V.D., was gazetted to command, bringing with him twelve Officers from his Citizen Force Battalion, the 56th (now 22nd) Battalion, C.M.F.—"The Yarra Borderers."

Immediately the C.O. arrived, the work of organising the 22nd Battalion, A.I.F., was undertaken with vigour. The Unit was then, and has continued to be (save for one Reinforcement draft) purely Victorian, and its members were drawn from all parts of the State. Most had received a good deal of Infantry recruit training, but a large number had been accepted as Light Horsemen, and their posting to an Infantry Battalion, instead of to a mounted Unit, was at first a keen disappointment. However, the decision of the authorities was accepted in good spirit, and the Battalion was the richer by the addition to its ranks of a very fine body of men.

The work of organisation and training was commenced at once. The monotony of Squad and Section Drill was relieved by occasional trips to Melbourne in train and charabanc, and by boxing and other contests held at the Camp stadium, where many fine contests were witnessed.

On 4th April, 1915, the first Battalion Parade was held, and Colonel Crouch made a spirited address, announcing "Wipe out the bloody Germans" as the regimental motto. The criticism of some prominent clerics, and the subsequent press discussion, served only to fix it more firmly in all minds. In the contracted form of "W.O.T.B.G." the motto was soon on all lips, and formed part of the chorus of the regimental song. The succeeding month was devoted to strenuous training in drill and musketry, and there were several ceremonial parades, including a Review by the Governor-General, Sir Ronald Munro-Ferguson.

Without any previous warning, the Battalion was one day informed that four days' furlough was available, and great was the ensuing commotion, as everyone prepared for final leave. Soon afterwards it was announced that the Battalion would embark on 8th May. On the evening of the 7th few men remained in Camp, and it was not until after midnight that the main body of the leave party returned, reflecting great credit on their drill instructors of the preceding weeks by the smartness of their parade under their "O.C."—Pte. Tom Moffatt. Marching through, they duly "eyes-righted" the sentries before being "dismissed" in front of the Orderly Room.

Next day, at 2.30 p.m., the Battalion marched to Broadmeadows Station, and entrained for Port Melbourne for embarkation on the transport "Ulysses" (15,000 tons). Nearly four years later, at the end of the war, a few original men made the return journey from England on the same boat. About 3.30 p.m. the pier was reached. A great crowd of relatives and friends had gathered to witness the departure, and progress from station to pier was difficult, even in single file. Many a man wondered at the host of friends who greeted him by name and wished him "Good Luck." Later, he realised that his "Sea Kit-Bag," with name conspicuously printed thereon, had played an important part. By 5.30 p.m. the 21st and 22nd Battalions, with 6th Brigade Headquarters, were aboard the "Ulysses," and the public were admitted to the pier. Half an hour afterwards the boat left. Lieut.-Colonel R. A. Crouch, V.D., was O.C. Troops on board, and Capt. A. R. L. Wiltshire Ship's Adjutant. The Battalion Transport Section did not leave until 9th July, on the "Hobart."

The Voyage.

That evening, pay was distributed, and—more important, as many found next morning—an issue of Sutherland's Pickles. At 10 a.m. on the 9th, the Heads were reached, and for the ensuing seven days, though the sea was calm, rations were plentiful, and "Fall in the sick" was an unpopular witticism. The "Euripides," conveying the 23rd and 24th Battalions, was soon sighted, and the two boats made the voyage together.

On the 14th, a last view was obtainable of the land to whose glory the Unit was to contribute in blood and lives—far, far more than entered the minds of those who that night watched its coasts slipping into darkness.

Next day, the first death on board occurred, and everyone was deeply impressed by the solemnity of the burial at sea. A Union Jack was the winding-sheet. Deceased had been a member of the 21st Battalion, and massed buglers sounded the "Last Post" with the two Battalions standing to attention.

The tragedy of the morning was forgotten later in the day, when a previously arranged programme of sports was carried out, concluding with an evening concert. Of this blending of death and gaiety, tragedy and mirth, there were later many striking instances.

During the voyage, the Battalion published a daily journal, which was appropriately enough named "The Odyssey." The publication was most popular, interest being sustained throughout.

A feature of the voyage, to be terminated only too soon by official intervention, was the shilling meal surreptitiously provided by a ship's cook.

Very early, there was heavy speculation on the Unit's destination. Egypt, Cyprus, and London were all well supported, with the last named a firm favourite. On 21st May, the Battalion Representative, Pte. Kruger—later awarded the D.C.M. on Gallipoli, and killed in action at Warlencourt—won the Lightweight Championship of the boat from Pte. Springhall, of the 21st, a boxer of some note. The first death in the Battalion was that of No. 207, Pte. W. A. Mathieson, of "A" Company, who succumbed to pneumonia, and was buried with full military honours on 22nd May.

Crossing the Line, the orthodox Neptune ceremony was held, with Pte. Val. Vousden, an entertaining ventriloquist, in the name part. He was assisted by Pte. Jim Lennie and Sgt. Reeve. Vousden was a man of over sixty. He had a keen sense of the dramatic, later strikingly illustrated on the eve of his evacuation from the Peninsula, when he insisted on being held up by comrades "to fire my last shot." They obliged the dying gladiator, whose premonition, however, was at fault, as he subsequently rejoined the Battalion, and served in France.

Before recording the arrival at Colombo, two other incidents deserve mention—the singing competition, wherein the Companies were placed "B," "A," "C," and "D," and the lazy-stick duel between Pte. "Jock" McIvor and a cook from the 21st, each winning a round. Betting on the final was heavy, and the Battalion held its first thanksgiving service when McIvor upheld its reputation and finances by pulling off the event.

Ceylon was sighted on 25th May, and the "Ulysses" anchored at

Colombo. Natives in their small craft immediately surrounded the ship, vending cocoanuts and bananas, which were hauled on board in baskets. One outstanding recollection of Colombo is that of a strenuous route march, devoid of liquid refreshment, which was undertaken on the morning of arrival. No evening leave was granted, but a few daring spirits slid down the ropes between ship and pier, and disappeared into the tropical night. The return was more difficult, and the case of Pte. J. D. Nicholson, the well known signaller and athlete, is the only recorded instance of a re-entry being gained by the rope which had provided such an easy mode of egress. The rest of the wanderers had, perforce, to mount by the gangway, where a Guard was waiting with an address book, in which many non-existent names and numbers were that night set down. The George Washingtons of the party were next day fined £5 each, and awarded twenty-one days' "C.B.," but later this was considerably modified. The net result of the jaunt and sequel was to reduce very much the profits gleaned from the lazy-stick competition.

Colombo has never yet appeared amongst the Battalion's Battle Honours, and it is for this veracious history to repair the omission. Leaving the Port, the Battalion gained its first victory against a barge, loaded with coal and niggers. The win was especially meritorious, in that for ammunition we had nothing more formidable than potatoes borrowed from the cooks, whilst our opponents used coal, until driven below by our fire supremacy. When out of range, they emerged like good sportsmen, and cheered the departing ship. Scarcely had the engagement been broken off when a tropical storm burst over the vessel, and the last memory of Colombo is of evening shades and pouring rain.

By wireless came fragmentary news of the 1st Australian Division's doings on Anzac, and on Sundays came plum-pudding for dinner. On 1st June, a monsoonal gale interfered considerably with the comfort of the Battalion, but next day the sea was unruffled, and Nature provided one of those never-to-be-forgotten sunsets, which were the perpetual delight of even the most unæsthetic.

On the 3rd, the "Ulysses" made the Gulf of Aden, and brought within view the towering cliffs of the Arabian coast, and a passenger vessel, with whose voyagers cheers were exchanged.

"C" Company were the Cricket Champions, and beat all opposing combinations. "C" and "D" N.C.O.'s disposed of those from "A" and "B". A very clever "Maud Allan" impersonation by Sgt. Rennie and Pte. Vousden won great applause.

Wireless news reached the "Ulysses" on 6th June of the loss at the Dardanelles of the "Majestic" and "Triumph," and on the 8th land was

Lt.-Col. R. A. Crouch, V.D.

everywhere discernable. About 2.30 p.m., the anchor was dropped a couple of miles from the shore, off Suez. A fleet of Arab boats, whose occupants sold Turkish Delight and postcards to the troops, was soon in the vicinity. That evening, the "Omrah" anchored close by, to the accompaniment of much cheering. Next day the Canal was entered. For this, some preparation had been necessary. As there was a possibility of being sniped at by Turks from the shore, steel plates and sandbags were taken on board, and cover was built round the bridge. No description could do justice to the first impression of the desert sands bordering the Canal, their barrenness conquered only by apparently endless stretches of telegraph lines. British and native troops were passed, and all semaphored "Good Luck."

There was still much speculation as to the Battalion's destination, but at 6 p.m. on the 9th the "Ulysses" reached Alexandria. On previous nights, no one had paid much attention to his toilet, but not so this evening. Shore leave was taken advantage of by most on board, and within a couple of hours only about sixty souls remained on the ship. Those who were present need no reminder of the small part the gangways played in this unofficial disembarkation. That night the 22nd Battalion made its first acquaintance with an Egyptian city, and tired parties moved boatwards from midnight until morn.

CHAPTER II.

EGYPT—JUNE-AUGUST, 1915.

About 9 a.m. on 10th June, 1915, the disembarkation of the Battalion commenced, and at midday it entrained for Zeitoun, via Cairo. The train journey was most interesting, and faster than some afterwards made in France. The harvest was being garnered, but the late crops remained untouched. Our troops were alert to notice the old-world methods of crushing corn, drawing water, and ploughing, also the entire absence of fences. For four hours the train traversed country where irrigation and intensive culture had, by centuries of toil, been developed to the highest stage of perfection.

The Battalion detrained at Zeitoun, and marched to Heliopolis. The men were soft from the long voyage, the packs and going were heavy, but no one fell out. Let a tribute here be paid to the spirit animating all throughout Egyptian marches. It was not fear of punishment, so much as the certain contempt and ridicule of their comrades, that stimulated the weary to the necessary effort. On this particular evening, however, none could repress a feeling of envy as the Battalion marched past Camp after Camp, and saw their occupants clad only in shorts and singlets.

Heliopolis Camp was well laid out, and every provision was made there for the troops' health and comfort. There were Mess sheds and Rest sheds, and the bathing facilities were of the best. The daily routine was as follows:—

> Reveille, 5 a.m.
> Morning Tea, 5.15 a.m.
> Parade, 6 a.m.
> Dismiss, 9.30 a.m.
> Lecture, 10.30 a.m. to 11.30 a.m.
> Dinner, 12.30 p.m.
> Fall in, 4.30 p.m.
> Parade, 5 p.m. to 7.30 p.m.

Slouch hats were now withdrawn, and this debonair headgear—the Australian soldier's most distinctive and highly-prized national emblem—was not re-issued until the departure for Gallipoli. Khaki shirts, shorts, and pith helmets were soon issued. They were more popular than the apparently never-ending inoculations.

Frequent visits were made to Cairo and Heliopolis; only for Cairo was a Leave Pass necessary. In this city of evil reputation there is much that is good and beautiful. To the loathsomeness of the native quarter, where men and animals herd together in filthy hovels, and humanity is to be seen in its grossest debasement, enough publicity has been given. Not so well known is the fascination and beauty of the real Cairo, that city apart, where East and West meet and mingle.

In its beautiful gardens a band played each evening to the crowd who strolled on its quaintly pebbled paths; there, too, could be seen many of our men, sitting at little tables sipping beer or eating ices, with an attentive waiter hovering always near, and often an obsequious guide, endeavouring to force himself upon the little party.

Entrance to a splendid Mosque, filled with rare treasures, could always be obtained, at a nominal charge for the slippers which prevented the Temple's contamination by the infidel feet of an Australian. From the ramparts around the Citadel a magnificent view could be had of the city, the river flats, and the Pyramids in the distance.

Cairo and Heliopolis were connected by an electric tram service, which, for speed and comfort, it would be difficult to surpass. The latter city was a picture of white and green loveliness, which had sprung into being only a few years before the war. Open-air entertainments with picture shows were a feature of its night life. These were liberally patronised by the men. The artists were mainly French, but an Australian occasionally braved the audience.

Interest in the natives, their customs and dress was intense. The appeals of the vendors of goods were couched in peculiar terms, and the paper-sellers contributed to the humour of the Camp. Units used them as carriers for their criticisms of neighbours and others. The results were sometimes startling. As an incitement to business, these were popular cries:—"Egyptian Timez—Very good news—Lord Roberts dead—Ten thousand Australians killed—Johnny Norton's paper." Other cries which are self-explanatory were:—"Eggs-a-cook"—"Eggs-a-fresh"—"Orangis, big, Two for one."

The wonder of the locality was "Sergeant McKenzie," an Egyptian kiddie, aged eight, whose uncanny knowledge of drill and rifle exercises astonished thousands. No movement was too difficult for him, and no problem of Guards and Sentries too intricate. For rifle, he had an airgun, and for bayonet a table-knife.

The natives did all cleaning and sanitary work, and sometimes accidents happened. Everyone will remember the case of the nigger who stole the washing. All the time the men were working hard to fit themselves for the strenuous days to come, and the effects of the training were daily becoming more apparent. A course of musketry was fired at Abassieh, half the Battalion visiting the butts at one time. In a shooting competition No. 8 Platoon were the winners. Night operations were more frequent than popular, and it was always a tired and thirsty Battalion that returned in the morning after a night on the desert. One morning a Sergeant accosted two exhausted Privates, dragging themselves back over the sand to camp, after just such a night. "Who are you, men?" he peremptorily asked. Aptly came the retort, "Burke and—Wills!"

The Battalion picnic to the Pyramids was an excursion to linger long in the memory. They were fifteen miles away, and at five one evening the Battalion set out with Colonel Crouch and the Band leading. Along the Mena Road the picnickers persevered, with the Pyramids always looming apparently just ahead. An adventure with a vendor of soft drinks and water-melons provided only temporary distraction. And still the Pyramids looked tantalizingly close. For hours the march continued, but just on midnight a halt was called on the site of what had been the 1st Division's camp, and a very light meal issued. Yet at midnight plus thirty there were countless Australians on top of the Pyramids. The gaiety was continued in the morning, when Church Parade was held in the shadow of the Sphinx. In the afternoon there were swimming races in the beautiful baths at Mena House. At 6 p.m. the "Fall in" was sounded, and the Battalion re-assembled. The journey home was by tram to Cairo, whence the tired picnickers marched back to camp. Everybody was more or less delighted with the outing, but none so much as those who had remained in camp!

During their stay in Egypt, everyone became familiar with the Egyptian patois, much of which was later transported to France, and some even assimilated into "Australian as she is spoke."

After the lamented death of Earl Kitchener, speculation was rife as to whether he had made any provision for the settlement by his estate, of the many tram and train fares charged against him while the Battalion was in Egypt.

About ten days before quitting Heliopolis, the Battalion received its first and second reinforcements.

At the end of August, camp was struck, kits checked, and the surplus returned to Giza, and after a night's bivouacking, the Battalion marched on the afternoon of the 29th through Heliopolis to Zeitoun, for an unknown destination. After a halt there of some hours, a train was

Lieut.-Colonel (later Brig.-General) R. Smith, C.M.G., D.S.O.

boarded, and, in crowded "dog-boxes," the Battalion journeyed to Alexandria. About 3 a.m. on the following morning, everyone was on board the "Scotian." Many a better ship has been torpedoed.

On 2nd September, Lemnos was reached, and news was received of the fate of the "Southland." A day was spent in the exquisite harbour, and swimming was permitted. The "Aquitania" was there, with a large number of British troops on board, en route for the Peninsula.

At 6.30 p.m. on the evening of the 4th, the "Osmanieh" pulled in and took the Battalion on board. Iron rations and ammunition had previously been issued, and, as firewood was reputed scarce, the containing boxes were broken up and carried forward. Submarine guards were plentiful, and stringent orders were issued against smoking and lighting matches. These were enforced by an Officer flashing an electric torch.

CHAPTER III.

GALLIPOLI—SEPTEMBER-DECEMBER, 1915.

It was shortly after midnight on 5th September, 1915, that the Battalion first sighted the ridges of Anzac, looming dimly through the dull light. A cruiser was firing broadsides into Achi Baba, and, as the transport drew closer, the sound of rifle and machine gun fire could be distinctly heard; a "demonstration" was in progress. An occasional flare or star shell pierced, but for a moment, the enveloping darkness, through which twinkled the lights from dugouts and shelters on the hillside.

In the bustle which accompanied the Battalion's transfer from the "Osmanieh" to two large lighters which came speedily alongside, there was little time for further contemplation. As the lighters were tugged to the beach, stray bullets droned by, and one wounded a private in "A" Company, the Battalion's first battle casualty.

A gentle night breeze carried from the shore the taint of a faint, strange odour, with which all were soon to become only too familiar; it came from the unburied dead of that heavy August fighting, which so nearly wrested the Peninsula from the Turk.

Guides were waiting on the beach, and led the Battalion by winding paths to Rest Gully, where the remainder of that night and the next day were spent.

The pack-drivers did not land on Gallipoli, but proceeded to Salonica with their horses, and subsequently participated in the Serbian campaign.

When daylight came, it disclosed an extraordinary sight in Rest Gully, for it was long after sunrise before the weary sleepers were astir. In many strange attitudes they lay; for pillows, some had used boxes of machine gun ammunition; others reclined on a comrade too sleepy to protest.

On 6th September, the Battalion relieved portions of the 6th, 7th, and 8th Australian Battalions, in the position opposite Johnson's Jolly, linking up with the Lone Pine defences, and commenced a tour of front line duty which lasted until the evacuation.

Before the tired veterans of the gallant 1st Division moved out, every available man lined the fire-step, and fired at Abdul a parting salvo of "Five rounds, rapid."

The appearance of the men of the 1st Division bore testimony to the hardships they had undergone. Their hair was long, their cheeks hollow, and their figures wasted by privation, fatigue, and scanty food. Many wore long beards and few clothes, and, indeed, looked very much the same as the men of our own Battalion were to appear before the evacuation took place.

Everyone soon became accustomed to the routine of trench life. For the first month, rations were adequate; afterwards, the state of the sea determined their quantity, and frequently their quality, as the bread often suffered from immersion in salt water. During the last month water was very scarce, and its issue had to be carefully regulated. At times the shortage was such that men ran alongside the pack mules, collecting the drips from the water-tins. "Beachy Bill" and "Asiatic Annie" soon introduced themselves, and the incoming of the barges under the former's fire became an anticipated spectacle. There were two other daily distractions—the glory of the evening as the setting sun illuminated Imbros, and contemplation of the "pretty" ship, as the Hospital boat was generally called. It was an appropriate adjective for the green-lighted, red-crossed vessel. On board this ship Major Derrick, O.C. of "A" Company, died from wounds within a fortnight of the landing. Capt. Curnow was thereupon transferred from "C" to "A" Company, to the keen regret of the former Company, for whose training and efficiency he was largely responsible. Major Conway commanded "B," and Major Mackay "D" Company. Capt. R. H. S. Abbott was O.C. "C" Company. His stirring lecture on the joys of Cairo, delivered to his Company before landing in Egypt, will ever be remembered by the original members of "C" Company. He was evacuated sick after a few weeks on the Peninsula, and did not rejoin.

On 18th September, the Battalion suffered a number of casualties from shell-fire, amongst them L.-Cpl. Moorhead, a Melbourne journalist, who lost a leg and his right arm.

The trenches were always kept scrupulously clean, and, though all the filth and refuse of "No Man's Land" lay a few yards beyond, not a match or scrap of bacon rind could be thrown down within. The Battalion's comparatively low sick-rate is ascribable to the strict sanitation enforced.

The end of September and beginning of October brought severe heat. Dysentery was prevalent, and the general health suffered. Clothing was reduced to a minimum, and many wore their equipment over bare skin. Others allowed luxuriant beards to grow, and youths acquired the appearance of patriarchs. Flies were plentiful and persevering, and it was difficult to convey food even from hand to mouth without their contamination.

Fatigue parties to and from the beach were an important and laborious feature of the life. They were philosophically accepted; one well-known C.Q.M.S. even found volunteers for these tasks, and explained his success in a sentence which became classic, "It's all done by kindness." The occasional lightness of the ration-carriers' burdens was atoned for by the magnitude of their "furphies." These varied from descriptions of hundreds of foreign Officers seen on the beach, to circumstantial stories of a relief by the Greek Army. Yet the first news of the evacuation came from Sikhs and Ghurkas, magnificent fellows who suffered terribly during the cold of November, and whose work deserves more kudos than it has yet received.

On 30th September and 5th October, the Turk assumed the role of "Demonstrator," but without causing serious damage. On 7th October, he caused great excitement by using what was believed to be a gas bomb. For some time thereafter, officers wearing red tabs haunted the bomb's resting-place, and as much care was taken in the excavation of its remnants as though they were relics from a buried city. The effective small box respirators were not then on issue, and the anti-gas equipment consisted of a piece of black gauze and a pad of saturated wadding. Very definite instructions were given as to the provision of a substitute should these be mislaid.

Flares were scarce, and their infrequent use an important event, preceded by a message passed along the trenches—"Mr. —— is about to fire a flare."

The first promotions to commissioned rank on the Peninsula were those of Sgts. Cawthorn, Sparrow, Rodda, and Peacock.

On 3rd October, elaborate preparations were made for the reception of a large number of Turks, who, for some reason, were expected to surrender in hundreds that evening. Sentries were carefully instructed to call out in Turkish—"Boori-yer-gal, Boori-yer-gal," when movement was heard in No Man's Land. Everyone played his allotted task except the Turks, not one of whom surrendered—possibly owing to the sentries' faulty accent.

During the hot weather, it was difficult at times to recognise the most exalted. One day an affable stranger met a party en route for the beach. "Going for a swim, boys?" he asked, and received an affirmative answer. "You often go for one, I suppose?" he continued. "Often, be

Sniper and Observer at Gallipoli.

damned. It's the first for three weeks," came the reply from a private, who failed to identify the shirt-sleeved enquirer as General Birdwood.

Opposite "C" Company's Sector was a crater, in popular estimation a veritable Turkish fortress. Every night movement was reported there, and "The Crater" attained a great notoriety, until a party consisting of Sgts. Stone and Turner (both killed at Pozieres) and Lieut. (then L.-Cpl.) Harold Smith, M.C., M.M., one night made a personal reconnaissance, and found it unoccupied.

Mail was delivered at regular intervals. After reading home letters, everyone turned to the Australian papers, containing letters from Officers and men on the Peninsula. These often contained amazing narratives of imaginary adventures and hairbreadth escapes, and greatly amused the troops.

The 20th October, a reputed Turkish Feast-day, was devoid of incident, but in the ensuing week all ranks suffered severely from cold and rain. On the 29th a regrettable accident occurred. About 3 p.m., a mine driven under the Turkish lines was "blown" under the supervision of Lieut. Bowra, an Engineer Officer, who, before the fumes cleared, went below, and was asphyxiated. Lieut. Thom, a fellow Engineer, who went to his rescue, shared a similar fate. Undeterred by these deaths, two Officers and a number of men from the Battalion entered the shaft, and worked at the recovery of the bodies. Two of them, Ptes. Good and Stelling, lost their lives at their voluntary task. Splendid work was done by the two Doctors present—Captains J. Fogarty and A. P. Drummond— and for their gallantry during the operations Lieuts. I. P. Stewart and E. T. Bazeley received Military Crosses. Distinguished Conduct Medals were awarded to Pte. Kruger and L.-Cpl. Stone, both of whom were subsequently killed in France.

The important events of early November were a Turkish "Demonstration" on the 4th, news of Patrobas' Melbourne Cup victory on the 6th, and the visit of Lord Kitchener on the 12th.

Activity on both sides was confined to mining and counter-mining, and the underground galleries and shafts were most intricate and interesting. The listening sentries could hear the Turkish miners working—the sound of their picks carrying through the sandstone. Several mines were "blown" by both sides, without much damage to either.

Sniping was reduced to a fine art, and Abdul proved himself a skilful and cunning marksman, excelled only by our own snipers, who were extraordinarily good. Cpl. Thurlow, of "C" Company (an old King's Prize-winner), and Pte. Ilett, "D" Company, proved themselves great

Turk-killers. Most of our casualties were head wounds, caused through sniping.

Lt.-Col. R. A. Crouch, V.D., who had commanded the Battalion since its formation, was, on 12th December, transferred to command the Mudros Base Camp on Lemnos Island. Major R. Smith thereupon assumed command, and piloted the Battalion through the remainder of its Gallipoli experiences and, with the exception of a very short period in Egypt, until his departure to command the 5th Brigade in December, 1916.

The end of November was bitterly cold, and, with bodies nourished on bully-beef and biscuits, and weakened by the monotonous diet, no one was in a mood to appreciate the snow-covered landscape; water was so scarce that snow had to be melted in biscuit tins; the machine guns were taken out of the trenches, and thawed at the cooks' fires. On the 29th came a few hours' intense bombardment from enemy naval guns in the Dardanelles. Lone Pine suffered most. Our Battalion casualties were comparatively few, but the Cemetery at Brown's Dip presented a depressing sight next day when the burials took place. The men's boots were now suffering from wear and weather, and frost-bitten feet caused some evacuations.

Early in December there were rumours of a relief, and when portions of some Medical Units departed, the old hands were convinced of "something doing." The secret of the evacuation was remarkably well kept, and the manner in which the arrangements worked reflects great credit on those responsible. The actual evacuation covered three nights. On the night of 17th December, the weakest men were sent off, and on the 18th about half the Battalion embarked without incident.

At 11 p.m. on the 19th the final evacuation commenced, and by 1 a.m. only a few picked men remained. The most elaborate precautions were taken to prevent the enemy guessing the truth. Every article of equipment that could creak or rattle was securely tied. Blankets, cut in strips, were swathed, moccasin-like, round the boots, and fresh earth was thrown along the hard trench floors to deaden the sound of retreating footsteps. The picked men remaining in the trenches continued sniping until the last. To Pte. "Barney" Horan fell the honour of being the last to leave his post, and his coolness and sang-froid on this occasion were later rewarded by the Distinguished Conduct Medal.

At 2.45 a.m., the last few men of the 22nd Battalion left the front line, first fixing rifles at the loopholes, with timed fuzes and an arrangement of weights, so that shots would continue to be discharged from the deserted trenches. The small party collected at the dressing-station, and with blanket-padded feet stole quietly to the beach. As the last party embarked on the waiting barges, the mine at Russell's Top was "blown," and brought on a heavy fire from the Turks, which soon settled down to the normal quietness of occasional sniping shots.

In darkness the Battalion landed on the Peninsula, and in darkness, and stealthily, it went away. No memory of glorious victory assuaged the universal sorrow at quitting the graves of those sterling comrades who were the first to fall. In the manner of their living and their dying these brave men founded our imperishable traditions, and that fine Battalion reputation which was never to be sullied.

During its months of hardship and anxiety on Gallipoli the Regiment had been tried and not found wanting, and its members sailed away, proud of having taken no inconsiderable part in what will go down to posterity as one of the most remarkable campaigns in the history of the war.

During its service on the Peninsula, the Battalion lost 616 in casualties, of whom sixty were killed, 285 wounded, and 271 were evacuated sick.

CHAPTER IV.

MUDROS TO MARSEILLES—DECEMBER, 1915-MARCH, 1916.

The manner of the evacuation had caused the Battalion's division into parties, some of whom went to the island of Imbros for a day. Within the next day or so, however, all were collected at Lemnos again, and, landing at Mudros, marched six miles over stony tracks to a camp at Mudros West. On the island there was an accumulation of Australian mail and, as there was no transport available, a volunteer fatigue party of some hundreds went in search of it and returned laden with thousands of letters and the popular Christmas billies. These were filled with good things, and did much to gladden the first Christmas spent abroad. Even the wrappers did their share, for on them was shown a kangaroo kicking a Turk off Gallipoli; below were the words "This bit of the world belongs to us."

The prevalent feeling was one of relief at again being free to walk and move without restrictions. Oranges were plentiful and a staple article of food, as fruit had been unobtainable for months. As plentiful, but more unpopular, were the speedily resumed route marches and drill. One day was given over to bathing in the hot sulphur springs at Therma.

With the New Year came the return into Egypt. On 3rd January, 1916, the Battalion boarded the "Ascanius," and on the 6th made its second landing at Alexandria. The transfer from the "Ascanius" to train for Tel-el-Kebir took only twenty-five minutes.

For some years there had been no rain at Tel-el-Kebir; this omission was rectified on the occasion of the Battalion's arrival. The few tents available were occupied by the 4th and 5th Reinforcements, who seemed reluctant to comply with the oft-repeated request of the bearded Anzacs to "make room for soldiers." Some of the quicker-witted secured ample space when they doffed clothes and initiated the newcomers into the mysteries of "chatting."

During the three weeks spent at Tel-el-Kebir the Battalion was present at General Murray's inspection of the 1st and 2nd Australian Divisions, who were formed up in mass and presented a magnificent sight.

Very little leave was granted, and few opportunities were available to dispose of the substantial paybook credit balances which had accumulated during the preceding months.

On the 26th January the Battalion entrained for Ismailia, and on the 29th marched to Ferry Post to relieve the 8th Brigade, another strenuous and well-remembered journey. The Suez Canal was crossed en route by a pontoon bridge. The transport section remained here, but the rest of the Battalion moved, after two days, to Brighton Beach, near Hog's Back, out in the wastes of Sinai desert.

The ensuing six weeks were very happy ones. Rations were good, and were substantially added to by gifts from the Australian Comforts Fund, to which the Battalion acknowledges a great debt of gratitude for a host of comforts supplied throughout the whole campaign. Two Companies were always on outpost duty, but this was not nerve-racking, as "No Man's Land" was many hundreds of miles wide.

A stadium was erected, and boxing and sports provided frequent distraction. Pte. "Snowy" Smythe, of "D" Company, was the crack pedestrian; Sgt. (then Pte.) McCormack, of "C" Company, who lost a leg at Bullecourt, and R. S. M. Porter, were prominent figures in the ring.

All water used in the camp was brought across the desert in "fantasses" by camels. These animals were even used as stretcher-bearers; quaint objects they looked with an arm-chair structure—fortunately seldom used—hanging on each side.

One day a new experience occurred in the form of a sirocco. During the morning the sky gradually darkened, until by noon it was almost black as night, and the wind, which at dawn had been but a breeze, increased in volume to a hurricane, charged with blinding sand, against which movement was impossible. When the storm passed the whole geography of the sand hills had changed.

On 8th March the Battalion arrived at Moascar, having been relieved by the New Zealand Mounted Rifles. The return march was not nearly so trying as the outgoing, as in the interim a road had been built.

During the ten days at Moascar there were many changes. A number of new Units were being formed, necessitating the transfer of many men from the Battalion, the strength of which was restored to normal by the return of convalescent sick and wounded.

Major Conway and Capt. Craig returned to Australia, and Lieuts. Roberts, Peacock, and Stockfield were transferred to the 5th Division.

Since the departure of Colonel Crouch, Major Smith had, except for a very brief period, commanded the Battalion. At Moascar, he was promoted to the rank of Lieut.-Colonel.

Lt.-Col. Norris, who had been with the Battalion for a few days at Brighton Beach, took over the command of a battalion in the 5th Division, and was subsequently killed at Fromelles, in France.

Sgts. W. Spiller and B. S. Tapner received their Commissions, and Lieut. Bird resumed Company duties, his place as Transport Officer being taken by Lieut. I. P. Stewart, M.C.

During the stay here the Canal was a popular bathing-place, and the Foden fumigator mangled the clothing for the first time, redelivering it to its owners in an entirely disreputable state.

There was much discussion as to the Battalion's destination. France was favoured only slightly more than Mesopotamia, and even India had some supporters, owing to some rupees having been distributed on pay-day.

The situation was still obscure when the Battalion entrained for Alexandria at 11.45 p.m. on 18th March. It had been a strenuous day. With General Birdwood, the Prince of Wales (then on General Murray's Staff) had reviewed the Brigade in the afternoon, and taken the salute in the subsequent march-past. When the parade was dismissed, the Prince made his way with difficulty through crowds of cheering men.

The troop train was made up of open trucks and, to everyone's annoyance, it rained again for the second time in seven years. The downpour was tropical, and there was no covering; it was a damp trainload that reached Alexandria at 7 a.m. on the 19th. The natives all knew that a move to France was in progress, and did a thriving business converting Egyptian coinage into gold.

By midday the train had pulled into the dockyard, and soon all were aboard the "Llandovery Castle," a fine ship, shared with the 2nd Pioneer Battalion, and a portion of the 6th Field Ambulance. This boat was afterwards converted into a hospital ship, and as such was torpedoed during the last year of the war, under circumstances which caused a world-wide outcry.

The Battalion transport had reached Alexandria, but embarked later on the "City of Edinburgh."

About 10 a.m. on the 20th the "Llandovery Castle" steamed out with Colonel Smith as O.C. Troops, and Capt. Bunning as Ship's Adjutant. After a day's rough weather the sea became calm, and the excellence of the food and accommodation made for a pleasant trip. The new Lewis guns, introduced at Moascar, were mounted by their crews under their O.C., Lieut. Harold Rodda, as a protection against submarines, which, possibly on this account, caused no trouble.

On the 23rd, the boat lay off Malta for some hours, but did not call. The beauty of the 24th was marred by a kit inspection, and next day

Marseilles Harbour was entered. Decks were crowded by men eager for a sight of France, and interested in the breakwater, the shipping activity, and the border of green which edged the shores—a refreshing and enticing sight to men who had just quitted the sands of Egypt.

The boat tied up about 3 p.m., and the unloading of the baggage was immediately commenced, but the troops were not disembarked until the afternoon of the following day.

It is, perhaps, unnecessary to record that shore leave was **not** granted on the evening of the 25th.

CHAPTER V.

THE FIRST MONTHS IN FRANCE—MARCH, 1916-JULY, 1916.

On the afternoon of Sunday, 26th March, 1916, the Battalion disembarked and marched through the manufacturing portion of the City to Marseilles Station. At 4.30 p.m. the troop train commenced its three days' journey.

Many hard, but true, things have been spoken and written of troop trains; this one proved to be the solitary exception. It was not crowded, there were actually carriages, and its comparative comfort added greatly to the pleasure of the journey.

First impressions, both of France and its troop trains, had afterwards to be modified.

The Rhone Valley was a thing of beauty. It was early spring, and the weather was glorious. The distant Alps made a hazy background, and white winding roads ran through trim vineyards, green long-grassed paddocks, and colour-splashed fields, of whose contemplation the eye never wearied, after so many weeks of Eastern desert life.

Ours was the first Australian Division to land in France, and the Battalion was feted at every stopping place.

The French Red Cross provided tea, and there were ninety-six hours rations on the train, but civilians loaded the men with wine and eatables. All they asked in exchange were "Souvenirs." "Souvenirs" and the gift of an Australian badge made glad the recipient. As the train approached the Capital, there were momentary fond hopes that it would pass through the City. The Eiffel Tower could be seen, but that, and a distant view of Fontainebleau Chateau and the Grand Palace at Versailles, were the only sights of Paris to be seen for many a day.

As the north was neared, the weather became showery and cold, and at 2 a.m. on the morning of the 29th March the train was quitted at Aire amidst sleet and snow, a sudden and startling contrast to the weather of Egypt.

Interpreters and advance officers were at the station, and led the Battalion on another of those long and trying marches to which reference has so often been made.

A Boxing Match at Hog's Back.

About 7 a.m. widely scattered billets were reached in and around Roquetoire. The intimacy of civilian billets was as much a novelty to the men as Australians were to the civilians, but an entente between ourselves and the French was here established, which has never since been broken. During the three years that have intervened, the latter have never tired of re-stating, "Australiens tres bons soldats," and we have continually paid our amazed admiration to their tenacity and cheery philosophy. In those days eggs and good champagne were cheap and plentiful, and the excellence of the French cooking caused a big demand for the former. The Battalion transport did not arrive for some days. From Marseilles they had gone to Abbeville, where they drew new vehicles and travelling kitchens, which they brought by road to Roquetoire; only the horses had accompanied them from Egypt.

On 31st March the Brigade was inspected by Lord Kitchener at Aire, and on 1st April P.H. gas helmets were issued, and instruction given in their use. It was generally felt, owing to some arrangements miscarrying, that an appropriate day had been chosen.

On the 4th the Battalion moved north from Roquetoire, and Haversque was reached on the first day, after a march of thirteen miles. The distance seemed like thirty miles to men whose feet, lately used to sand, were now jarred by cobbles.

Next day's stopping place was between Sailly and Estaires, a fifteen mile trek, finished with swollen feet and unlaced boots.

A great reception had been accorded the Battalion as it went through the villages, and everyone suspended work to watch the column pass.

On the night of 7th April the Battalion carried out its first relief in France, taking over the Reserve Line at Fleurbaix from a Battalion of Suffolks. Elaborate precautions, which a year or two later would have caused hilarity, were taken to avoid noise and lights.

The vivid and continuous illumination of the front line by German flares was of particular interest to those who, on Gallipoli, had been compelled to report every light fired. They sincerely hoped that the same trench standing order was not in vogue in France.

After eight days in reserve, the Battalion relieved the 21st Battalion in the front line, then a quiet place.

"No Man's Land" varied from 100 yards to 400 yards in width, and all dangerous spots in the breastwork trenches bore notices such as "Do not loiter here," "Fixed rifle on this spot."

Casualties were light in this quiet sector. Pte. R. Jordon, of "C" Company achieved the melancholy distinction of being the first member of the 22nd to be killed in France. Our patrols soon came into collision with the enemy, and, in a night encounter, Lieut. J. C. McCaul was seriously wounded and did not rejoin the Regiment again.

Additional reinforcements under Lieuts. Fussell and Fraser here joined the Battalion, and Lieut. Miles replaced Lieut. May as Q.M., which position he filled with much ability until the Battalion's demobilisation.

Trench mortars were not then well understood, and the first Battalion demonstration was hardly a success.

The first mortar bomb struggled into "No Man's Land," and the next burst over our own lines, but an urgent message prevented further trouble.

Gramophones became suddenly unpopular. One was taken to a salient for a joke one evening, and rendered the "Turkish Patrol" to applauding Huns. An encore number, "The Stars and Stripes," to the accompaniment of machine gun fire and "five rounds rapid," brought hundreds of flares and retaliatory shelling later in the evening. It is doubtful who scored the honours.

Early in May the Brigade went into reserve, and the Battalion into billets and huts near Erquinghem, then a nice village, very close to the front line, but practically undamaged, and with its factories working. In one of these were excellent baths.

There for six weeks we trained and did fatigues, journeying to and fro in full marching order to wiring and digging tasks.

The Battalion was also submitted to the camera for the well-known picture "Happy Australians," and to an inspection by the Hon. W. M. Hughes and the Hon. Andrew Fisher. The latter's white flannels made a great impression on the troops. The same evening everyone had to march five miles to work on digging trenches. It was a day of mixed blessings.

There was much laying of cables and digging of reserve lines, but the commencement of limited English leave opened a brighter vista.

Steel helmets and box respirators were not plentiful, but in May portion of the Battalion was provided with both.

Two Officers were killed on detached duty—Lieut. Bruce King by hostile shell fire, and Capt. H. Buckley, the original Adjutant, in a bomb accident at Fleurbaix. The latter had been wounded on the Peninsula, and only rejoined on the day prior to his death.

On the evening of 10th June the Battalion relieved the 28th Battalion in the Bois Grenier reserve line, remaining there for more than a week and eventually moving into the Rue du Bois salient.

The salient itself was subject to both enfilade and frontal fire, and the Company that held it suffered one half of the heavy casualties resulting from this tour of front line duty.

FIRST MONTHS IN FRANCE—MARCH, 1916-JULY, 1916

Lieut. Oldfield was killed, and Capt. Davis and Lieut. Cawthorn wounded. The latter made an unexpected recovery, rejoined the Battalion, in which he did much useful work, became a Captain, and later transferred to the Indian Army.

The shelling was heavy on both sides, and aerial torpedoes and minenwerfers added to the troubles.

On 26th June the Huns put down a particularly heavy bombardment, in which Armentieres suffered; splendid work in maintaining communications was done by Lieut. L. A. McCartin, M.C. (then a L.-Cpl.).

A Brigade raiding party of 200, to which each Battalion had contributed an equal quota, had been for some time in training near Armentieres under Capt. A. R. L. Wiltshire. Raids were still a novelty on 29th June, when, under a heavy artillery and trench mortar barrage, the raiders rushed the German lines. In the main, the raid was highly successful, and about eighty Germans were killed or left for dead, while a number of prisoners were brought back for identification and information. Our own casualties did not exceed fifteen. For his services Capt. Wiltshire received a Military Cross, and the specially good work of Stretcher-bearer "Red" Strain brought him the M.M. Amongst the wounded were Lieuts. Hunter and Fussell. The latter was invalided to Australia; the former returned to the Battalion, obtained his captaincy, and was again wounded while in charge of "D" Company during the attack on Ville-sur-Ancre, in May, 1918.

The Battalion was relieved next evening by the 23rd Battalion, and on 3rd July the sector was handed over to the 3rd New Zealand Infantry Brigade.

The night of the relief was marked by an intense bombardment, which caused several fires in the billets the New Zealanders had just quitted. The roads were weirdly lit up by this conflagration.

Shortly after midnight the Battalion commenced its march through Steenwerck to La Becque, a pretty spot, where a stay of four days was made.

The Somme offensive had now begun, and it was generally known that the Battalion was to move south and participate. Everyone was in high spirits, and the grim Pozieres drama cast no premonitory shadow.

The departure from La Becque was a minor tragedy, for there was not enough transport available to carry the accumulated impedimenta; in consequence, many a French household became the richer by a discordant gramophone or a set of crockery.

After a night at Fletre the journey was resumed. Lunch was taken at Hazebrouck, where the kindly townspeople filled the streets and gave gratuitous refreshment to all.

Renescure, with its good billets, was reached on 9th July. Here Lieut. I. P. Stewart became permanent Orderly Officer, and shortly afterwards Adjutant. He retained this position until incapacitated by wounds in August, 1918.

Reveille on July 11 was at 2 a.m., and St. Omer Station was reached at 7.30 a.m., after a four-mile march along the well-known canal. At 8 a.m., the train for the south steamed out. It passed through Calais, Boulogne, and Etaples, to Amiens, traversing a countryside whose summer loveliness made everyone realise the beauty of invaded France. As the train passed Ailly-sur-Somme, a few made casual note of the name. But when they detrained at Amiens, and found that a ten-mile march back to that village lay before them, there were many deep and fervent curses bestowed on the war, the staff, French troop trains, France, and, above all, on the unfortunate little hamlet.

The route for the march lay through the historic city of Amiens, soon to become familiar to all, but only a glimpse of its magnificent cathedral could be obtained. Closer inspection of this and other beauties of the capital of Picardy and the Somme had to be delayed until following days, when leave was granted.

O.G.1. Pozieres.

CHAPTER VI.

POZIERES—JULY-AUGUST, 1916.

It is not easy to write the story of Pozieres, the bloodiest and most costly battle in which the Battalion was ever engaged. There had been a series of attacks prior to its entrance, which coincided with the maximum concentration of hostile artillery.

Neither the Germans nor ourselves had yet adopted the system of "defence in depth," and the battle zone contained far more men than two years later would have been employed. On these an unceasing hail of shells took heavy toll. Though a mantle of peace once more envelops the world, it is, perhaps, unwise to attempt too minute a description of the awful scenes enacted there. Only the word-pictures of a Zola could truthfully paint their ghastliness. In Pozieres sleep more of our Brigade than in any other spot in France, and the casualty list of this Battalion was the heaviest in the Brigade. It might well be so, for the 22nd lost thirty-three officers and 763 men. The enemy was determined, by prodigal expenditure of the lives of his picked troops, to arrest our advance. The number of German dead lying on the battlefield proved with what resolution they fought.

A fortnight elapsed after its arrival on the Somme before the time came for the Battalion to play its part. The first four days were spent at Breilly, in drilling, route-marching, and swimming. Then came short stays at Rainneville and Puchvillers; the last parades before the great battle were at Lealvillers, where there was another halt of four days.

Early on the morning of 25th July the march to the line commenced. The route lay past the ruins of Albert, from whose shell-wrecked steeple the leaning statue of the Virgin looked down upon the moving Companies. The Brickfields were reached before breakfast. All packs were dumped here, and fighting order was assumed. Everyone carried, in addition, a circular tin disc, to facilitate identification by our aircraft; it is doubtful if this experiment was a wise one. It was here, also, that news was received of the 1st Division's successes. In the fields round Albert their battered Battalions were sleeping. They had just emerged from the line after their capture of Pozieres village, and their appearance recalled memories of a previous meeting on Gallipoli.

That evening the Unit relieved the 6th Battalion, moving through the notorious Sausage Gully, where guns were massed wheel to wheel, and care had to be taken in passing to avoid injury from their "flash," past the Chalk-pit, into hastily constructed trenches beyond the village. "D" and "C" Companies occupied the front line between the cemetery and what was once a fruit garden, and "A" and "B" Companies were in Kay Sap. The enemy guns were exactly ranged, and the shell fire now experienced was a dreadful illustration of scientifically organised barrages. When one lifted, another commenced. High explosive shells blew in the crowded trenches, filling them with earth, and wounding and burying many of the garrison. The 21st Battalion, who carried forward the rations, and subsequently took over this sector, were also heavy sufferers in the inferno.

During the four days the Battalion held the line, another Brigade made an unsuccessful attack on a strong trench system known as O.G. 1 and O.G. 2, in which "D" Company of the Battalion took part. Under Major M. N. Mackay, they reached the German wire, and, with the few available shovels and their entrenching tools, were digging in, when, owing to the failure of the major operation, they were ordered to withdraw. This they did, under cover of a fog.

Kay Sap received both enfilade and frontal fire; it had no fire step, and was continually blown in; in the debris dozens of our men were buried. Gas shells added to the horror, and for four days none slept. During one period of two hours the Battalion stretcher-bearers alone carried out 126 men. Though the weather was hot, the dead could not be buried. The shells, malignant and relentless, killed wounded and buried living and dead together. Through this inferno men worked and carried, or, what was harder, only waited in the tortured sap for a shell which was inevitably to come upon them. The most amazing feature of these days was the alacrity with which men volunteered for almost certain death. No task was too dangerous to deter them, and those who knew became for all time convinced that the Australian soldier was without an equal.

The "runners" were supermen. Sometimes two would be struck down within sight of the trench they had quitted: without order or invitation, their places would be taken by comrades, who had seen their fate, and yet volunteered to tilt with death.

In Kay Sap, Lieuts. Hart and Tapner were killed; the firstnamed had joined the Battalion only two days before his death. The wounded in sap and front line included Captains Andrew and Wiltshire, and Lieuts. Frazer, Bunning, Bazeley, and Allan.

The bombardment on the night of 29th July was so intense that the relief by the 21st Battalion, which commenced at 10.30 p.m., could not be completed until dawn. The Battalion then moved back to Sausage Gully, and during the next five days reorganised and "rested" in the scanty intervals between fatigues. Another attack on O.G. 1 and O.G. 2 had been decided on, and the fatigues included the digging of a jumping-off trench, or "J.O.T.," within 300 yards of the German lines.

Immediately prior to this attack eleven 2nd Lieutenants were commissioned, viz., 2nd Lieuts. Thomas, Condon, Yeates, Yeadon, Scanlon, Kennet, Kellaway, Scammel, Handasyde, Blanchard, and King. Within forty-eight hours of receiving their commissions, the first-mentioned six were killed, and the next three wounded; of the remaining two, Lieut. Blanchard was severely wounded at Mouquet Farm, but Lieut. King served with the Battalion until the last fighting before being wounded and invalided home. He and Lieut. Handasyde, who was invalided to Australia after Pozieres, are the only two of the eleven now alive. Lieut. Scammel was killed at Bullecourt in May, 1917, and Lieuts. Kellaway and Blanchard at Ypres in October of the same year. At the same time and place Lieut. Skene-Smith was killed. He and Lieut. Kellaway were the recipients of the only two Military Crosses awarded for the Pozieres operations. Could there be a more striking illustration of the terrible price exacted by the war from our infantry?

The attack on O.G. 1 and O.G. 2 was timed to commence at 9.15 p.m. on 5th August. "B" and "D" Companies were to capture the first, and "A" and "C" the second objective. These Companies had been reinforced during their stay in Sausage Gully by a number of 9th Reinforcements, who played a splendid part in the subsequent fighting. They moved from Sausage Gully by platoons at 5 p.m., and filed into Dinkum Alley. Where the Alley ended was an open space, which had to be crossed to reach Kay Sap, Tramway Trench, or the J.O.T. It was in Tramway Trench that "A" and "C" Companies were to await zero hour, and then move through the J.O.T. and O.G. 1, on to O.G. 2. The entry into Dinkum Alley had, apparently, been observed by the enemy, who put down a terrific barrage upon it and its exit. The congestion was beyond description. Other Battalions were moving at the same hour, and men would follow guides, who had shouted "'B' Company this way" or "'C' Company will move back," only to discover, after a long interval, that the Companies directed were of another Unit. Up and down the Alley the stragglers wandered, and, in the confusion, men and hours were lost.

Before the attack commenced, the Companies had lost by shell fire 20 per cent. of their personnel. It was impossible for those in charge to entirely sort out their commands from this tangled mass, and precious minutes were slipping by. Sgt. Bregenzer, who won a Distinguished Conduct Medal in October, 1917, at Broodseinde, and was killed at Herleville in August, 1918, did valuable work here. Taking up a position in the open ground at the exit, he encouraged and directed the men towards the J.O.T., and, although in the most exposed position, himself escaped injury.

When the attack barrage opened at 9.15 p.m., only about thirty men were in position. At 9.25 p.m. this number had greatly increased, and at 9.30 word came from Major M. N. Mackay, who commanded "D" Company, and had done magnificent work in bringing it into position, that all available men had arrived.

Owing to the heavy losses, Major L. W. Matthews, who supervised the forward arrangements, decided to eliminate one of the originally proposed two waves, and at 9.31 the order to advance was given. "A" Company of the 23rd Battalion, who simultaneously gallantly endeavoured to secure the left flank, were practically annihilated by machine gun fire.

Before O.G. 1 was reached, Major M. N. Mackay and 2nd Lieut. Pritchard were killed, and 2nd Lieut. W. S. Wolff was wounded. The command of "D" Company then fell to 2nd Lieut. R. Blanchard. There was not a great deal of hand-to-hand fighting in O.G. 1 itself, as our barrage had killed or wounded most of the enemy there, and smashed their entrenchments, and within a few minutes it was securely held by the attackers. A dugout which caught fire resisted all efforts to extinguish it, and provided a beacon light for runners throughout the night. One does not like to think of the fate of the many German wounded who filled this and other dugouts. The number of their dead and wounded lying hereabouts spoke volumes for the desperation with which the enemy had fought to retain these commanding positions. "A" and "C" Companies had shared in the shelling and confusion of the early evening, but the greater portion of them reached Tramway trench, from which they moved forward in attack formation to the J.O.T., entering the latter as the first two Companies quitted it.

The original plan was to push forward without a halt, but the events of the night made it necessary to pause on the J.O.T. for a few minutes to reorganise. They then continued the advance to O.G. 2. This was not an organised German line of defence, and what trenches there were had so suffered from high explosive that their very existence was difficult to determine in the darkness. But the position of the barrage and fragments of German wire helped the Companies to locate themselves, and they dug in.

The 7th Brigade had linked up on the right, but the left, which

Mouquet Farm

swung back to O.G. 1, was unprotected and raked by machine gun and artillery fire. This was the dangerous flank.

Early in the morning a few hardly spared men from O.G. 2, under Sgt. Selwyn, commenced the digging of a Communication Trench to O.G. 1, but with dawn came a German barrage and counter-attack. Nowhere did it break our line. On the unprotected left the attackers came within bombing distance, but in no single instance did they reach the trench. Our casualties were heavy, particularly from snipers, who had crept forward to cover the attack. It was by one of these Capt. Curnow was killed.

Every officer in O.G. 2 was now a casualty except Lieut. Harold Rodda, who not only remained there until relieved, but did exceptionally good work in all the Pozieres and Mouquet Farm operations, without receiving a wound. It was in O.G. 2 that Ptes. O'Neill and Weston won their D.C.M's. The latter was shot through the head and blinded. Though in agony and minus an eye, he clung to a Mills bomb from which the pin had been withdrawn until it was taken by comrades. To his D.C.M. was added later the Russian Cross of St. George.

All through the day of 5th August the shelling continued without ceasing, and dead and wounded lay in heaps together. At times the trench held hardly a single unwounded man; once it was thought that all were killed, but at intervals others were dribbled in from O.G. 1.

Nothing could be done for the wounded for the time being. Later, German stretcher-bearers and our own worked side by side, and collected those who were still alive.

In spite of stubborn fighting the line held, and on the evening of the 5th-6th the remnants of the 22nd Battalion were relieved by the 24th, and moved back to Sausage Gully, and next day to Tara Hill. Only four unwounded "Company" officers remained.

Where so many suffered and died, it is invidious to comment on men or officers, living or dead. But amongst the latter were two of the Battalion's senior and best known officers, Major Murdoch Mackay and Capt. H. F. Curnow. Both were Bendigo men. The former had, after a distinguished University career, practised as a barrister in Melbourne. He left with the Battalion as a Captain, and received his majority on the Peninsula. By his high personal character, his keen sense of justice, and undoubted military ability, he had gained the respect and confidence of all ranks.

Capt. Curnow had, in his time, commanded two Companies. When on the Peninsula, he left "C" Company to take command of "A," his departure was for long a matter of regret to his old Company. His return to the Battalion after a fortnight's illness was the occasion for a unique demonstration of affection. Though his own standard of life was a model one, he combined with it a tolerance and understanding which endeared him to all, and won him a universal popularity.

The work of a Company Officer, Lieut. Rodda, has already been spoken of. A tribute is due to that of the Medical Officer, Captain Craig (afterwards Major Craig, D.S.O.), and Chaplain Captain Durnford (afterwards Major Durnford, M.C.). The former organised parties of stretcher-bearers, and shared their dangers. When no more than a percentage of the wounded could be brought to him, he went forward to O.G. 1, and there did all one man could do to alleviate their sufferings.

The story of Capt. Durnford's work had been many times re-told. He fell in with ration carriers and stretcher-bearers, working unceasingly for the living, and insisting on reading, under heavy shell fire, the burial service over the dead. He was from that time onwards a well-known figure throughout the 2nd Australian Division.

Space does not permit the mention by name of the many brave N.C.O.'s and men in the ranks, whose courage and cheerfulness proved a wonderful inspiration and aid to the officers. It was the fine individual work done by our splendid private soldiers and N.C.O.'s that carried the Regiment through.

So ended the first week at Pozieres. The Battalion was to engage in many another strenuous fight, but the rigours of that time have never been, and never can be, repeated.

CHAPTER VII.

MOUQUET FARM—AUGUST, 1916.

Although the Battalion had suffered so heavily, further hard fighting was to be expected. The reception of reinforcements to fill the depleted Companies, and the organisation of specialists, became the first concern. It was only possible to allow about fourteen days' respite in all, and most of this was spent on the march.

From Tara Hill the Battalion moved, via Albert and Warloy, to Berteaucourt, which was reached on 10th August. At Vadencourt Wood, on the 9th, a halt was called, and the left of the road was lined—on the right was a portion of the 1st Division returning to the battle—as His Majesty the King drove by. The same night the Battalion bivouacked in La Vicogne orchard, resuming the march next day to Berteaucourt, where billets were good and the villagers most kind. Nearly two years later many had an opportunity of revisiting this village, and the pleasure of renewing acquaintance with old friends there.

During the outward march, and at Berteaucourt, the Battalion obtained many new officers to replace the recent casualties. From the 21st came Capt. Crowther and Capt. Harold Smith; from the 23rd, Capt. J. M. Main and Lieut. W. A. Cull; the 24th gave Lieut. Cumming and Lieut. Hughes, M.C.; and all officers who had been attached to other Units were recalled. Lieut. R. P. Penna was transferred from the 1st Division, and Sgts. J. H. Evans, L. A. McCartin, N. W. McCormack, and A. W. Smith received their commissions. Sgt. W. C. Greig received his shortly afterwards.

Only eight days could be spared for re-organisation, and the training of Lewis gunners and other specialists was energetically proceeded with.

On the 18th August, the march to the line re-commenced, and La Vicogne orchard was again the night's resting-place. It rained heavily, until everyone was saturated and anxious for dawn, but the weather was equally bad for next day's march to Herissart. On Sunday, 20th August, Contay was reached, and that afternoon, after Church parade, General Birdwood presented decorations won by members of the Brigade. On the Monday, after an early reveille, the Battalion reached the Albert brickfields, where a very cold night was spent, and on the 22nd August re-entered Sausage Gully.

Three Companies, under Capt. Cull, lived among the chalk-pits, and carried bombs and rations forward from the dump there. "B" Company were first employed on road building, and later were attached to the 21st Battalion for the impending attack on Mouquet Farm.

Shelling was heavy on the 23rd and 24th August; on the 25th Scottish troops succeeded in an operation on the left, the 6th Brigade's attack was fixed for the 26th. Many of the bitterest struggles of the war were fought for a few yards of ground, the possession of an old ruin, or a piece of trench of no value tactically, and important only as indicative of a victory gained and a foe vanquished. More often than not, the maintenance of a gain like this was a costly encumbrance. It cannot, perhaps, be said that Mouquet Farm was without tactical importance, and its defences were certainly of an intricacy that was not disclosed until the first attacks were made, but there was nothing in the appearance of the ruins to suggest that their possession was worth, or would entail, a pitched battle. Yet Mouquet Farm was not taken till almost a Division had been thrown against it. The title of "Farm," however appropriate it may once have been, was at this time almost a cynical misnomer. Shells had for long been the only plough to furrow its lands, the bodies of the dead were the only seed strewn, and the earth grew nothing, although watered with a rain more precious than any other it had known.

Around Mouquet Farm was a system of cleverly constructed tunnels, precursors of those to be later embodied in the Hindenburg line, of which the attackers knew nothing till the enemy appeared in positions where none had been before, and molested flanks from which resistance could not have been anticipated.

The 21st Battalion bore the brunt of the 6th Brigade's attack on 26th August, but it is to the events of that day, as they concern the 22nd, that this chapter must be confined. "B" Company's mission was to move forward at zero hour, 4.45 a.m., into shell holes on the left of the main attack, which flank they were to protect. Under a good barrage, the Company left its trench in Indian file, and wheeled by platoons in the desired positions. Capt. Harold Smith and Lieut. N. L. Cumming, who, with Lieut. Harold Rodda, were the officers in charge, led Nos. 5 and 6 platoons to link up on the objective with the 21st, but a nest of German gunners at the junction point caused heavy casualties. Capt. Smith was soon wounded, but continued to do splendid work till he was killed. Lieut. Cumming penetrated to the objective with the handful of men who had survived the enemy fire, and fought a bombing action until he was severely

Zonnebeke, J.O.T., 4th October, 1917.

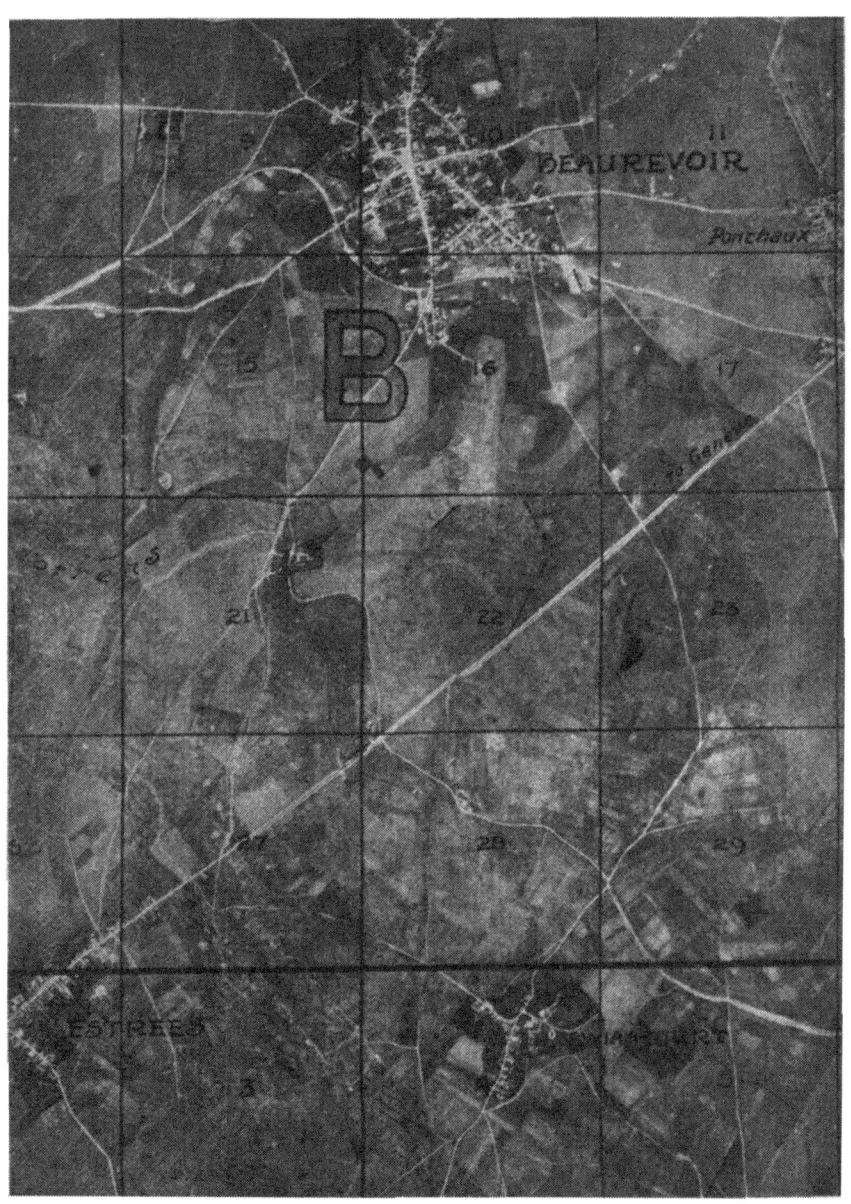

Aeroplane Photo. of Beaurevoir Battlefield.

wounded. Being then unable to regain our lines, this officer was taken in by German stretcher-bearers, and it was not until 1918 that he was repatriated.

As in O.G. 2, on 5th August, Lieut. Rodda was the only unwounded officer, and he assumed command of the Company. Hostile artillery was now heavily shelling the main attack, which met with a stubborn resistance, and was confronted with the cunning tunnel defences, of which mention has been made. By means of these, the 21st Battalion was attacked in rear, and almost hemmed in. Not only were their losses very heavy, but it was impossible to clear the ground of wounded. Owing to their flank position, and the fact that theirs was a shell hole, and not an organised trench line, "B" Company of the 22nd escaped with lighter casualties than at one time seemed probable, and the survivors maintained their allotted flank until relieved at 2 a.m. on 27th August.

Prior to the attack, "A" Company, under Lieut. McLellan, had moved to Tom's Cut, and throughout the day "C" and "D" Companies were employed carrying. When the main attack proved unsuccessful, all available men took up a position in First Avenue, and in the evening "C" Company relieved "A."

Mouquet Farm was not to fall to our Brigade, but was only carried after repeated attacks by another Division. Early on 27th August the 22nd Battalion was relieved by the 14th Australian Battalion, and, organised as two Companies, marched in pouring rain to the outskirts of Albert, where billets were found for the night.

CHAPTER VIII.

YPRES—SEPTEMBER-OCTOBER, 1916.

The Battalion had suffered so by the Pozieres fighting that a move to a quieter sector was obviously imminent.

Warloy, Rubempre, Fiefes, and Gezincourt were the first stopping places. At Fiefes, General Birdwood again reviewed the Battalion, and thanked it for the magnificent work lately performed. On moving from Rubempre, the packs were carried—a red letter day.

After two days at Gezincourt, a short march on the morning of 5th September brought the Battalion to Doullens, where it entrained for the then more tranquil north, arriving at Proven about 9 p.m. On detraining an eight mile march had to be undertaken to Eyrie Camp, where the blankets which had been handed in on 1st July were re-issued.

This was the Battalion's first visit to Belgium, and the flat, damp, and uninteresting country proved a great contrast to Picardy.

It was not possible at the time to erect a memorial to the men of the Battalion who had fallen in the great Somme battle, but the matter was not forgotten.

Through the courtesy of the 6th Field Company Engineers a massive cross was afterwards built, to which was affixed a splendid brass tablet made from German shell cases, bearing the Battalion colours and a suitable inscription:—

Erected by their Comrades of

22nd AUSTRALIAN INFANTRY BATTALION.

In Loving Memory of

The BRAVE OFFICERS, N.C.O.'s, and MEN

of the REGIMENT,

Killed in Action at

POZIERES and MOUQUET FARM,

25th JULY-27th AUGUST,

1916.

For the first nine days in Belgium only the mornings were devoted to drill; the afternoons were given to sports, and leave could be obtained to visit Poperinghe. This pleasant interlude was of short duration, and on 14th September the train was taken at Vlamertinghe for the ruins of Ypres.

Though the sad fate of this town has raised it to an unhappy eminence and its ruins have acquired a melancholy interest, there is, for the soldier, little to distinguish it from any other town of the devastated area. To the poet and the artist he leaves the lamentation or the rhapsody: his chief concern is to find a decent billet.

In Ypres, cellars in the Convent sector were used as billets by the 22nd and 23rd Battalions alternately for the next five weeks.

The ruins were lightly but consistently shelled, and in October a few casualties were suffered there by the Battalion.

The 22nd and 23rd Battalions now shared the line work of the Brigade on this front, relieving each other at seven day intervals on a quiet sector near Hooge. Its right flank rested on Sanctuary Wood, and its left on the Menin Road. The tranquillity was marred by large rats which infested the trenches, and by larger minenwerfers.

Major H. A. Crowther now returned to his old Battalion, the 21st., and Captain A. R. L. Wiltshire, M.C., now recovered from wounds, on returning from hospital, received his majority, and became the Battalion's second in command.

Captain J. S. Dooley (later Major Dooley, M.C.) joined here, and took over "C" Company. He was soon known by, and immensely popular with, the whole Battalion.

On the 19th October the return journey to the Somme commenced.

The series of great battles, which commenced on 1st July, still continued, and the Battalion was to take a hand in the concluding phase of the 1916 offensive.

After two days in Ottawa Camp and re-crossing the frontier into France, brief halts were made near Steenvoorde, Buysschure, and Nortleulinghem.

On the evening of the 24th, a troop train was boarded at St. Omer Station, and early next morning the Battalion detrained at Longpre, near Amiens, and marched to excellent billets at l'Etoile, on the banks of the Somme.

The next move introduced novel transport, motor-busses belonging to the French Army carrying the whole Battalion to the Sugar Factory at Ribemont, whence it marched to Buire, and commenced its experience of the desperately long and rigorous Somme winter.

CHAPTER IX.

WINTER ON THE SOMME—NOVEMBER, 1916-JANUARY, 1917.

The great offensive had not yet finished, but the first weeks of a winter of unparalleled severity necessarily entailed its conclusion. These are days of evil memory to the Battalion, for the mud and wretchedness of Flers sector, where many of them were spent, cannot be pictured in a description in which convention limits the expressiveness of the adjectives used.

The four days at Buire were wet, but it was not until 2nd November, when the tour of line work began, that the depths of misery were plumbed. Before moving up Sgts. K. S. Anderson and L. W. Harricks received their commissions.

No other mud has ever attained so evil a notoriety as that of Flers; it was of a consistency, depth, and stickiness unequalled by anything afterwards encountered in Flanders. Enemy shell fire was frequently heavy; at Factory Corner, Lieut. N. W. McCormick was killed.

In the Flers sector every phase of winter weather was experienced—rain, snow, sleet, and frost—and this November no one cared which horse had won the Melbourne Cup. There was even here a grain of comfort in that everyone was too weary to worry much about the numerous shells, which stimulated the prevailing hilarity.

No more opportune time could be selected for a word of praise to the Transport Section, their horses and mules. Theirs was an unhappy lot, for the least deviation from the tracks which passed for roads meant disaster, and the almost certain loss of an animal. On occasions the main road was littered for miles by vehicles which could not be extricated from the mire. The work of stretcher-bearers, never easy, became intolerable. There were cases where relays of carriers took six and seven hours to convey a wounded man over the short distance between the front line and the forward dressing station. "As bad as Flers" has been adopted as a standard description of any scenes of peculiar filth and wretchedness.

It was for work in this sector that Major Dooley received his Military Cross.

Lieut.-Colonel A. R. L. Wiltshire, C.M.G., D.S.O., M.C.

On 14th November the 5th Brigade made a successful attack, and on the 15th the enemy retaliated with many gas shells.

The 19th brought a relief, and on that day the Battalion handed over to a British unit the mud, slush, and goodwill of this very vile locality. The ordeal of moving out from the line over many kilometres of squelching mud devoid of duckboards, was an ordeal never to be forgotten by the weary men who laboured for hours in the quagmire. A laborious journey outwards was the inevitable sequel to every tour of duty. The assistance received on these occasions from the "Y.M.C.A." by our almost-spent men cannot be exaggerated. Their "soup kitchen" was the goal towards which all persevered; after a halt and refreshment, the final stage would then be undertaken.

Without desire to engage in any controversy, and prompted merely by a sense of justice, another debt must be acknowledged—to that much maligned beverage, rum.

Four nights were now spent in huts near Fricourt, and the following days were given to the removal of mud from the adjacent roads.

It was here Lieut.-Col. R. Smith, who had commanded the Battalion since Egypt, and received as its Colonel the D.S.O., left to take temporary command of the 6th Brigade. He was subsequently appointed Brigadier of the 5th Brigade, with which he gained great distinction.

Major A. R. L. Wiltshire, M.C., assumed temporary command of the Battalion, a position he retained until the end of February, 1917.

The last days of November were spent at Dernacourt. Immediately on its arrival there the Battalion was inspected by a Divisional General, and its mud-stained appearance ovoked some comment; from the nature of its recent labours, some signs of wear and the Somme winter might almost have been expected.

The inspection took place on ground inches deep in snow, and its conclusion met with the hearty approval of all ranks, who by that time were chilled to the very marrow.

On 1st December, Flesselles was reached, after a railway journey as slow as it was cold, but the seventeen days spent in this village were as pleasant as days could be in the winter season.

The men were re-equipped, and enjoyed excellent Christmas dinners. These anticipated the Christmas season, which was spent in the front line.

On 3rd December, General Birdwood attended a Brigade church parade, and distributed decorations.

On the 17th, the Battalion moved by train to Ribemont. Reveille that morning was at 5 a.m., and the station was reached at an early hour, but it was only after a tedious wait and a return march to billets for dinner, that the train pulled in.

The reinforcement draft which now joined did not participate in the Ginchy tour of duty, but spent a month at Bussy-les-Daours in further training.

On Christmas Eve the Battalion went into the Ginchy sector. The best that can be said of Ginchy is that it was better than Flers, but even Ginchy had no asphalt pavements.

Christmas dinner in the line was of bread and bully-beef. The weather was bad, and though battle casualties were not heavy, the novelty of the strenuous conditions was responsible for a number of cases of "trench" feet. It was only by continual massage, frequent changes of socks, and the unremitting attention of platoon commanders, that this complaint was mastered.

The Ginchy sector probably still holds many an unsalvaged trench boot, which sunk in Needle, Spring, or Cow trench, and stayed there despite the struggles of its wearer.

The Battalion cooks and Q.M.'s staff worked very hard to alleviate these bad days, and if the inventor of "Tommy Cookers" ever needs a testimonial, he may refer for it to these pages.

The sector will long live in the memory of our transport section. The dreadful weather and exposure, coupled with heavy work, made demands on strength and endurance that cannot be imagined by those who were not there. For the work done by the stout-hearted boys of the Transport during these hard times there can be no praise too high.

Altogether there were three tours of front line duty here, at four-day intervals.

Our artillery ushered in 1917 by hurling many tons of shells on the German lines as a New Year's gift.

The night of 16th-17th January saw the commencement of the long frost, which lasted for six weeks, and introduced a new problem. Whereas previously it had been difficult to raise mud-laden boots from the ground, care had now to be exercised to maintain a footing on the frozen earth and duckboards.

On 18th January the Battalion was relieved, and moved to Ribemont for ten days. "Coming out from Ginchy" is a phrase provocative of many recollections.

Even in peace days Ribemont had never been a fashionable winter resort, but cold and poor though the village was, the rest there revived many a man who had been tried almost beyond endurance.

Again must mention be made of those magnificent private soldiers, who proved themselves as indomitable and philosophic in the trials of this winter as they had previously been in burning desert sands and during the hardships of Gallipoli.

The socks and comforts provided by the Battalion's many good friends in Australia did much to ease their hardships. To the 6th Brigade Comforts' Fund special thanks are due.

Capt. Bunning and Lieuts. Alderson and Woolf, who had all three been wounded at Pozieres, now returned, and Lieut. Massie rejoined with his commission from an Officers' Cadet Battalion.

At the end of January the Battalion moved via Becourt and Shelterwood Camps to the Le Sars sector, facing the famous Butte de Warlencourt.

The land was gripped in an iron frost, and the shell-pitted region was no longer a sea, but a field of ice many feet thick, which men dug out with picks, and carried in sandbags to struggling fires, where it slowly melted.

The icy temperature was agonising on feet and fingers, and, although the long darkness, broken only by vivid gun-flashes, was unutterably wearisome, the prospect of a thaw was appalling. No one wanted a recurrence of Flers and Ginchy. Yet it was so cold that the moistened hair froze as it was brushed, and bread had to be thawed at a fire before it was cut. The earth was void of vegetation, and the few surviving bare dry branches were as ghosts of happier days.

In the third week of February the thaw commenced; as the month was dragging to an end the snow melted, and the forward area was a semi-frozen muddy sea, where movement was difficult, and every shell-hole a trap for the stumbler.

In the last week of the month, Lieut.-Col D. M. Davis received command of the Battalion, then manning a line of outposts facing Warlencourt. This was the position on the eve of the Battalion's relief, when sudden orders were received at 11 p.m. on 24th February to issue S.A.A. and bombs, and "prepare to advance."

CHAPTER X.

THE GERMAN WITHDRAWAL—FEBRUARY-APRIL 1917.

It is difficult to express the general amazement when the startling order to advance was received on 24th February, for it was unthinkable that an ordinary attack would be launched so unexpectedly, or indeed, at all, under the prevailing conditions.

As "C" and "D" Companies, who, under Lieut. E. T. Bazeley, M.C., and Captain W. A. Cull respectively, constituted our front garrison, were being hurriedly organised for the advance, news came that patrols on the battalion's right flank had found portions of the German front line unoccupied, and that a general enemy withdrawal was suspected.

Some time after midnight the two Companies moved off towards their objective, Gallwitz Trench, a broad, creek-like excavation, knee deep in mud and devoid of habitable dug-outs, which lay between our posts and the village of Warlencourt, and had, up to this time, served as the German front line. There was no barrage, and the strange advance, made in darkness over unknown country abounding in shell holes and wire, was the Battalion's initiation into the tribulations of "peaceful penetration." The trench had been abandoned by the enemy earlier in the evening, and was reached and occupied without opposition. At dawn, patrols pushed through the village of Warlencourt without establishing contact with the enemy. Captain Cull then went forward with one scout only, and succeeded in reaching Malt Trench, and carried out a most daring and dangerous reconnaissance.

Throughout 25th February hostile field guns were active against the new positions, but caused very few casualties. In the afternoon orders came that Malt Trench was to be occupied at dusk. This trench ran along the crest of a hill beyond Warlencourt, and was well protected by rows of wire. It was apparently thought that no more opposition would be encountered than on the preceding evening, for not more than 100 men from "C" and "D" Companies undertook the attack, which was made without artillery support on a frontage of nearly a mile. At 5.30 p.m. these men began the ascent of the hill: "C" Company were on the right, and passed through Warlencourt; "D" Company were some distance further

Chaplain-Capt. F. H. Durnford, M.C.

left. As "C" Company moved out of the ruins, a number of Germans could be seen on the summit of the hill, and a terrific volume of machine gun fire swept the hill side. At the same time, and in response to flare signals, enemy field guns and mortars put down a barrage. Even those engaged in the attack remarked the number and variety of the multi-coloured flares. To those who regarded it from afar the display looked extraordinarily beautiful. In these circumstances, the attack was foredoomed, but the attackers pushed on to the uncut wire, through which impenetrable barrier no further progress was possible. "D" Company suffered most heavily, for portion of the enemy trench system provided shelter on the right.

Lieut. W. Corne was killed, and Capt. W. A. Cull, a most courageous and capable officer, was severely wounded, disabled, and caught in the wire. He was taken in by the Germans, and, after many months in hospital, was repatriated.

Amongst the casualties was No. 2151 Sergeant J. Harwood, who behaved with great gallantry until wounded, and was later awarded the French Croix de Guerre.

The total casualties during the tour of duty amounted to about sixty.

The ground was a quagmire, and all ranks were exhausted when, next day, the postponed relief took place, and the Battalion marched to Shelter Wood Camp for a rest of four days. This camp was a collection of huts, which reared themselves from the slime of the Somme. They were huts and nothing more, without chimneys and, in many cases, deficient in lining boards, which "previous occupants" had used for fuel.

It was part of every platoon commander's duty to prove conclusively, by a careful check of the remaining boards on his platoon's arrival and departure, that the responsibility for the damage lay on "previous occupants." Yet the Battalion's "rests" in this camp after tours of line duty were always eagerly anticipated.

Malt Trench had been captured prior to the next visit to the line, and after a few days at Le Barque Switch the Battalion moved into it.

Throughout his retirement the Hun's policy was to man selected spots as strong posts, and hold them with machine gun crews. These posts were often scattered along a continuous trench, all protected by wire, and were very hard to locate; patrolling was more than ordinarily dangerous.

It was on work of this nature that Lieut. H. V. Massey was engaged when he met his death in front of the then uncaptured Grevillers line. He had, as a stretcher-bearer, won a Military Medal at Pozieres.

The weather was bitterly cold, and the fighting was still in an area blasted by our shells and German malignancy.

The Australian battalions have always been prepared to ungrudgingly acknowledge what merits the German possesses as a fighter, and our tribute to the methodical manner of his retirement would be unqualified had the Hun only been a sportsman; but we have never yet been able to dignify him with that title. It was not that we expected him to delay his departure to establish clubs for our officers, or Y.M.C.A. huts for our men, nor did we look for furnished apartments in his evacuated villages. We were prepared to see in every undestroyed dugout a potential death-trap, and not to query his right to poison the wells, but we did think he might have spared the peasants' fruit trees.

From the sight of so much destruction it was a relief to turn to the work of our own Engineers. The speed with which they laid down a light railway was indeed amazing.

After many days in Malt Trench and Layton Alley, the Battalion marched out one evening to Bazentin Camp. The journey was probably not much more than eight miles, and even though the inclement weather had played havoc with the roads, the slowness of the weary men's progress gave them a better view of the guns, waggons, and limbers which impeded the route.

Bazentin was reached about 2 a.m. At 8 a.m. the serenity of the sleeping camp was disturbed by an order to "Fall in and move up again."

With great expedition the sleepers rose, and were soon retracing the miles so wearily toiled over on the preceding night. At least one man missed his breakfast, the exquisite pleasure of this early morning outing making an indelible impression.

Eaucourt, l'Abbaye, and Le Barque were the first places garrisoned on reaching the advanced lines again, and daily progress was made on the heels of the retreating Boche.

The 23rd Battalion were the first to enter Bapaume on 17th March. Fighting was still progressing on the outskirts, when bands of souvenir-hunters and "ratters" from the 22nd Battalion entered to see what could be picked up.

The Battalion was then on the left of that town and in front of Grevillers, whence a move was made to Ravine Gully. Here Lieut. E. T. Bazeley, M.C., whose work on Gallipoli has been previously mentioned, was transferred to the 23rd Battalion as Adjutant. He received his captaincy immediately, and later became a staff officer with 2nd Australian Division.

On 22nd March snow—and Prince Eitel Friedrich of Prussia—fell. A foolish attempt to escape from his fallen aeroplane cost the Prince his life. While attempting to regain the German trenches on foot he was shot by a member of the 23rd Battalion.

THE GERMAN WITHDRAWAL—FEBRUARY-APRIL, 1917

Early on the morning of the 26th, "B" and "C" Companies moved into Bapaume, to billet in the Town Hall. But in the brief interval between the departure of its late occupants and the arrival of our companies, the establishment was blown up by an ingenious clockwork mine left by the Hun. Instead of finding the "home" they had been looking forward to, the companies were given the task of shovelling the Town Hall off the road.

Two days later the Brigade was relieved, and the Battalion moved into hut shelters at Mametz Wood. Parades were resumed, and Mametz will always live in our history as the spot where Battalion drill was brilliantly executed over shell-holes, roads, and barbed wire entanglements.

Early in April it seemed that the Battalion's mission was nearing an end. News of America's entry into the war was followed by accounts of a great Canadian victory at Vimy Ridge. On our own front, the enemy had gone back to open country, and touch was just being established along the Hindenburg line.

These high hopes were not realised, but the war news of the day was a splendid tonic after the drudgery of the winter, and all ranks were in splendid spirits.

On 13th April a move was made through Bapaume to Beugnatre, where the night was spent; next evening the Battalion took over the line on the left of Moreuil.

On 15th April the Hun made his unsuccessful and terribly costly attack on Lagnicourt. This village lay beyond our right flank, but the Battalion Lewis gunners promptly doubled into range, and did great execution on the flank of the advancing waves of field-greys. A party of one officer and eleven men who attempted a raid on one of our posts were all killed, and for his work Lieut. F. Gawler received a Military Cross.

Fourteen German battalions took part in the main attack, and their dead was conservatively estimated at 1500. It was the 5th Brigade, then commanded by our former C.O., Brig.-Gen. R. Smith, C.M.G., D.S.O., which inflicted most of this drastic punishment.

The record of the morning would be incomplete without mention of the dash shown by the Battalion cooks and cookers who ambled into Noreuil, headed by the Transport Officer, Lieut. Evans, and found the Hun in temporary possession.

The middle of April was wet and cold, and the last night of the tour in the line a nightmare; everyone was drenched, and all the fragile shelters were swamped. The attack planned for this time was postponed, and the 5th and 6th Brigades were now relieved by the 7th, who held a two-brigade frontage.

The Battalion went to Favreuil, commencing an elaborate course of training, and every morning gained brilliant victories over an imaginary enemy. The daily objectives were invariably captured with such facility that quite a lot of time was available for sports.

The weather was making a tardy atonement for its previous vagaries, and even the shell-holes were responding to the advent of spring.

A Battalion sports meeting was a great success; there were frequent football matches, and the Divisional Canteen, under the management of an officer of this Battalion, was only a few hundred yards away.

On Saturday evening, 28th April, the whole Battalion was alarmed by a midnight order to "man the Corps line," and in more or less haste, according to the hour of their retirement and the strenuousness of their day, all ranks "stood to."

When the last man was in position, the "dismiss" was given, for the call out was purely experimental, and the time taken by various officers and companies had been carefully "clocked."

In meditative mood, and with caustic comments on the peculiar notions of humour that the army nourished, the Battalion went back to bed. The Q.M., Capt. Miles, broke all records for rapid turnout on this occasion.

On 26th April the artillery commenced a preparatory bombardment of the German lines, and on the evening of 2nd May the Battalion moved to a gully in rear of the front line, and to the right of Bullecourt.

No praise is too lavish for the excellence of the arrangements made for that night by the Battalion's administrative staff.

The many articles necessary for the morning's attack were drawn by platoons systematically and speedily, and some hours were available for sleep before the Battalion was awakened to line the J.O.T.

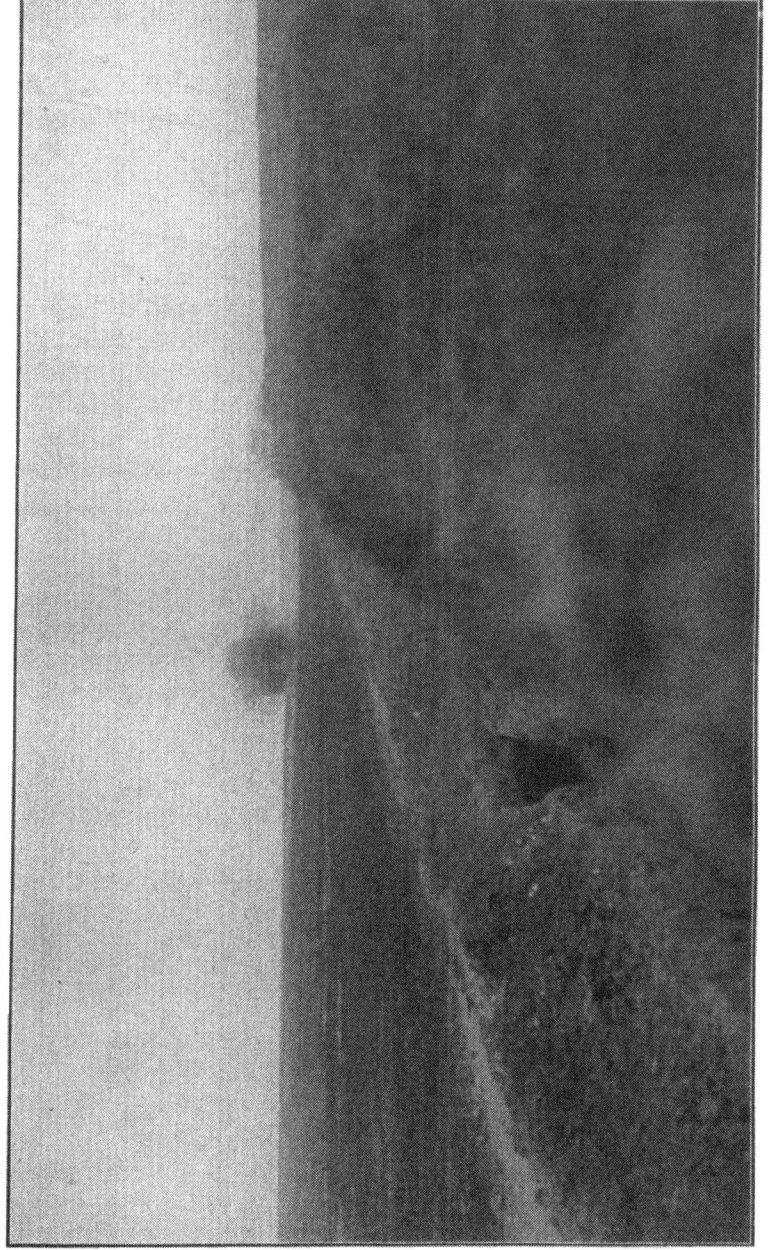

Bullecourt Battlefield.

CHAPTER XI.

BULLECOURT.—MAY, 1917.

The Battle of Bullecourt occupies a unique place in the Battalion's annals. For no other struggle had the preparations been so complete, the rehearsals so thorough, or the general organisation so apparently perfect. Yet, within a few minutes of its commencement, the combat developed into a pell-mell of violent hand-to-hand struggles, where the 6th Australian Infantry Brigade met the flower of the German Army, and beat it into quiescence.

Every initial advantage lay with the enemy. The vaunted Hindenburg line was on ground of their own choosing; from the whole of the occupied area they had selected it, and for months had laboured there with an enslaved civilian population, to construct an impregnable barrier. This they had succeeded in doing to their own satisfaction. The best engineering talent in their army had sited the machine gun positions with carefully designed and intersecting arcs of fire, through which they had deemed it impossible for attackers to pass. Elaborate care had been taken to reduce losses from the barrage which would precede an attack, and shell-proof dugouts, easy of access and exit, were provided for their garrison.

More important than all else, the enemy had secured reliable and detailed information about the impending attack, and knew the calibre of the troops who were to make it on the Bullecourt sector. The Kaiser himself had reviewed the picked battalions who constituted its garrison, and specially commissioned his "beloved Cockchafers" to repel the attacks to be made by the Australians, to whose fighting qualities, as captured documents later showed, he made complimentary reference.

The village of Bullecourt lay slightly to the left of the sector where the Brigade attacked; to the north, the German defences ran in an almost straight line to the Arras-Douai railway; at Croiselles and Bullecourt they bent and ran back towards Havrincourt Wood. It was of the greatest importance to the enemy that this bend, on which both sections pivoted, should not be pierced, as it was a keypoint in the Hindenburg line.

But it was pierced, taken, and held by the 6th Australian Infantry Brigade.

Zero hour was fixed for 3.45 a.m. on the morning of 3rd May. On the right the 5th Australian Brigade, and on the left the 62nd British Division, were to make a simultaneous attack.

The early morning hours of that day were lighted by a moon whose rays enabled the blurred outlines of moving figures to be discerned even at a considerable distance, but the ten minutes immediately preceding zero hour were of an intense darkness.

The "J.O.T." was parallel to the enemy lines, and 500 yards in front of a steep railway embankment. In a fragile shelter, under the partial protection of this embankment, Brigadier-General J. Gellibrand, C.B., D.S.O., had established his forward headquarters, and there he remained under the heaviest shell-fire, and in intimate touch with every development throughout that and the succeeding day. To his virile leadership and active command the success of the operation may be largely attributed.

No modern battle can be accurately described in detail, for survivors' impressions are drawn from purely personal experiences within a limited area. This is peculiarly true of the events of 3rd May. It was, in every sense, a Brigade, and not a Battalion, battle, where, in at times almost chaotic confusion, men of all four Battalions were often joined in one bombing party; and splendid services were rendered by the Brigade Trench Mortar Battery.

As the units filed over the embankment to form up on the "J.O.T." in the respective "waves" to which they had been allotted, the moonlight apparently revealed them to a suspecting enemy. Searchlights and flares made movement difficult, and though the shells and minenwerfers which commenced to fall did not prevent the ordered formation in "waves," they caused frequent casualties. For about ten minutes before zero hour the hostile barrage was very heavy.

At zero our own artillery opened, and the advance began. Very little distance had been traversed before a concentration of shells, minenwerfers, and machine gun bullets fell upon the Battalion's centre, and caused its casualties to substantially exceed those of any other in the Brigade.

The intensity of the hostile machine gun fire has, fortunately, not been equalled in any other of this Battalion's experiences. The noise of the bullets and the rattle of the machine guns that strewed them were distinct sounds, that rose above the din of the barrage.

The 21st Battalion also lost very heavily at this stage. The survivors pushed magnificently onwards, but no longer in the systematic waves of a few minutes before, and the battalions blended.

Our left and smaller party almost immediately encountered severe resistance, and did not completely attain their objective, which was on the

Brigade's extreme left. They were not in touch on the right, and on their own left no progress whatever had been made by the English. In this critical position they received enfilade and frontal fire from a resolute enemy, but established themselves in shell-holes just short of their objective, and carried on a musketry duel until dusk.

The right and main body followed closely on the barrage, and gained the German line, where they commenced a bombing action which lasted for twenty-four hours.

The remaining waves, in conjunction with the other battalions, continued the advance to the second German line, from which, despite the formidable resistance of a large garrison, our "Success Signals" were fired at 4.26 a.m. On this objective's right flank another bombing action now began, and continued incessantly for five hours.

The position after the first two hours may be briefly summarised as follows:—The 6th Brigade had established itself in both the first and second systems of the Hindenburg line, and for some distance further forward, where the gallant work of our comrades of the 24th Battalion was especially notable. On its left, the German positions were entirely maintained. On its right, all but a portion of the first German trench line was still in the enemy's hands.

Throughout the day counter-attack followed counter-attack. They numbered thirteen in all, but the renowned "Cockchafers" and Prussian Guardsmen found that in the men of this Australian Brigade they had more then met their match. It may be recorded with just pride that not in one single instance did any of these desperate counter-attacks succeed. The enemy displayed great enterprise and daring, exposing himself freely to secure better targets, and the question of our ammunition supplies soon became serious.

These had to be brought overland through intense barrages and under heavy machine gun fire. One "carrying party" of thirty, under Lieut. Filmer, was reduced to four, when he led its remnant to the objective. Within a few minutes he himself was killed.

The casualties among our stretcher-bearers were extremely heavy, and no praise is too high for their work and that of the A.A.M.C. attached.

At 8 a.m. the situation was most critical, as at that hour the Brigade was completely hemmed in, and with very limited supplies.

Midday brought better news from the flanks, but more determined counter-attacks. Not only were these gallantly repulsed, but in the afternoon a resolute attempt was made to take the whole of the frontage originally planned "so that a completed task might be handed over to the relieving Brigade."

But it was difficult enough to obtain sufficient bombs to maintain the ground held, and none were available to repulse the counter-attacks vigorously made against the new gains.

The 23rd and 24th Battalions had held the right flank all day against many counter-attacks, prosecuted with renewed vigour towards evening. This they continued to do, despite any successes gained by the enemy against units who intermittently established themselves on the Brigade's right flank.

From 7 p.m. to 10 p.m. the Brigade was again isolated in the line and on the railway embankment in rear. A heavy barrage fell for hours, until a weary enemy's efforts slackened and died. By evening it was evident that the enemy on this sector was drubbed to a standstill, and that he recognised his inability to match the troops he was up against. The prisoners who fell into the hands of the Battalion were of a particularly fine type, and belonged to picked regiments who had received special training.

Between midnight and 4 a.m. on the 4th the 1st Australian Brigade took over the sector, and the next twenty-four hours were spent by the Battalion along the railway embankment, whence, on the morning of the 5th, a shift was made in small parties to the Noreuil sunken road. Owing to the severity of its losses, the Battalion was acting as a Company, with each Company as a Platoon.

It is impossible to enumerate the many gallant N.C.O.'s and men lost by the Battalion at Bullecourt. Their names are, unfortunately, too numerous to receive the individual mention each deserved.

In twenty-four hours the Battalion had lost sixteen officers and 422 other ranks, of whom over fifty per cent. were "killed" or "missing." Though no other battalion in the Brigade lost so heavily, the day's fighting cost the four battalions fifty-eight officers and 1422 other ranks.

Captains J. H. Slater and E. G. Hogarth, and Lieuts. S. Scammell, H. P. Fraser, W. S. Filmer, and J. Griffin were killed in the attack, and Lieut. W. C. Greig died of wounds sustained in the Noreuil sunken road during preliminary operations.

There were many wounded officers, of whom four, Captains L. Elmiger, W. Spiller (then Lieutenant), Lieuts. Wicks and Bennett were invalided to Australia. Many of these left Australia with the Battalion, and the names of all are familiar to those who have served with it. To those of their own time their merit was personally known, and to their successors their deeds have been often retold.

Captains Slater and Hogarth were particularly well-known. The former had for years been one of Geelong's most prominent footballers. Captain Hogarth's demeanour a few minutes before his death has often

A Little Game.

Officers, June, 1918.

been spoken of by the survivors of his company. When the German barrage fell on the troops lying on the "J.O.T." he calmly walked up and down in front of his men, encouraging everyone by his extraordinary sang-froid and example.

The decorations for Bullecourt included Military Crosses for Chaplain Captain Durnford and Lieut. W. Mc. Braithwaite.

The former, repeating his deeds at Pozieres, did invaluable work amongst the wounded.

Lieut. Braithwaite, though wounded on two separate occasions, persevered to his objective, and most resolutely led a bombing party against a troublesome enemy machine gun. This brave officer later became a company commander, and survived many another battle, only to meet his death in the Battalion's last fight at Beaurevoir, a month before the armistice was signed.

The struggle at Bullecourt will always live in our annals as a costly and bloody battle, brought to a successful issue by the courage and endurance of the men of the Battalion and the Brigade. It is with a sincere wish to add to the knowledge and pride of those who cherish the memory of the men who fought and fell there that the story of Bullecourt has here been written.

CHAPTER XII.

BULLECOURT TO BROODSEINDE.—MAY-SEPTEMBER, 1917.

Pleasant Days.

The period of over four months that lay between the battle of Bullecourt and the Battalion's entry into the third battle of Ypres was devoted to hard training and thorough reorganisation. So long an absence from front line duty was neither expected by us nor desired by the Higher Command, but the unsettled weather of the 1917 spring altered many plans, and added considerably to our "rest." It is now generally known that the army declines to accept the dictionary interpretation of the verb "to rest," and our work throughout the four months was very strenuous. During the concluding weeks an unhealthy competition (from the view point of all except mounted officers) sprang up between various Brigades and Divisions, who sought to emulate each other's performances in long distance marching. Yet it must be admitted that our recollections of the time are, in the main, very pleasant indeed. This does not, however, apply to the commencing days of our rest, for the night of the 7th May was very wet, and the consequent relief and move to Favreuil made a wretched finale to the Bullecourt fighting. Through one of these unfortunate, but possibly inevitable, accidents which happen even in the army, there was no camp available for the Battalion's accommodation, and all ranks spent the night without cover and in teeming rain.

Next day the journey to Mametz camp was commenced. The men were carried in trucks on a trench railway, which ran from Bapaume to Le Sars. After a night under canvas at Le Sars, the Battalion moved on the 9th May, via Martinpuich and Contalmaison, to Mametz. It was there our popular Doctor, Capt. W. B. Craig, received his majority, and Sergt. G. T. Burrage was commissioned.

On 17th May the Battalion left Mametz, and marched via Aveluy to Bouzincourt. Pleasant spring weather and an attractive countryside added greatly to the enjoyment of our month in this village. A number of men were sent to a seaside camp to recuperate, and football and sports provided abundant recreation. A very successful Brigade sports meeting was held on 30th May, a nice fresh day, when an excellent programme was terminated in the early evening by a series of spirited boxing contests.

While the Battalion was here Lieut.-Colonel D. M. Davis left to take command of a Training Battalion in England.

Lieut.-Colonel Davis was a man absolutely imperturbable under fire. After the Bullecourt battle he was surrounded by the survivors of his officers in the Noreuil sunken road, when a low flying Hun aeroplane swooped down on the party, and made play with its machine gun. Not unnaturally, the group dispersed in some haste. Only the Colonel remained upright and impassive. His comment was characteristic: "Too late, too late, forty-five yards away now—forty-five yards away."

On 6th June General Birdwood and the Hon. Andrew Fisher were present at a Brigade Church Parade, and after the inevitable speech making the troops marched past.

Promotions were numerous owing to the Bullecourt losses. Lieut. H. C. Rodda now received his Captaincy, and shortly afterwards Lieuts. H. J. Sparrow and W. J. Cawthorn were promoted to the same rank. C.S.M. J. McIntyre was made a 2nd Lieutenant.

On 15th June the Battalion entrained at Varennes for Bapaume, whence it marched to Beaulencourt, there forming portion of the Divisional Reserve for the Corps in the front area. It was a tedious day, for enemy aircraft had damaged the railway line, and some hours elapsed before the train could proceed.

Major A. R. L. Wiltshire, M.C., was now promoted to the rank of Lieut.-Colonel, and assumed command of the Battalion, a position he held throughout the remainder of the campaign, and until the Battalion was finally returned to Australia.

Major L. W. Matthews returned to the Battalion from detached duty, and became second in command; and a number of junior officers were taken on strength from Cadet Battalions. Amongst these were 2nd Lieuts. K. Sutherland, E. Thewlis, and N. H. Dooley.

At no stage of its history has the Battalion participated in more "tactical exercises." Nearby was the ruined village of Villers au Flos. This unhappy spot was attacked by us at all hours and from every angle—on one occasion with "tanks," represented by hessian screens, in charge of Lieut. C. J. Fulton. It was with much interest we read of the capture of this village by the French during the 1918 offensive.

Reveille was always at an extremely early hour, and there seemed to be no end of the combinations of which we were invariably a part.

When we had done our duty as a Battalion we became portion of an attacking Brigade, and when this idea had been exploited we were allotted a new role in Divisional manœuvres. It is idle to pretend that all ranks shared in the zeal of the higher command, and even the occasional change of locality to Le Transloy did little to ease the heartburnings. Everyone expected an early "real" attack. Interest in the offensive had been transferred to Belgium, where the "quiet sector" of 1916 was now the scene of much preliminary activity, and news of our move thither was daily expected.

On 24th July the trek began. The route lay through Le Sars and Pozieres, past the familiar battle grounds of the 1916 winter and spring, where every spot evoked reminiscence, and many of them are forever enshrined in Australian tradition.

It was almost the first anniversary of Pozieres, and as, at midday, the Battalion passed the two memorials erected on the battlefield to the memory of the fallen of the 1st and 2nd Australian Divisions, there could be but one common thought.

The noon halt was within a few yards of Gibraltar, into whose depths many wandered. Nearby was the cross erected to the memory of our Battalion officers who fell at Pozieres.

The march was resumed along a dusty road until the outskirts of Aveluy were reached, and the backwaters of the Ancre came in sight. The opportunity of a dip after a hot march was too good to miss, and the Battalion swam en masse.

It was while at Aveluy that the Brigade lost the services of Brigadier-General J. Gellibrand, C.B., D.S.O., who left to assume a command in England. He later returned to France, and became a Divisional Commander.

The long expected move from the Somme took place after a spell of four days in a camp at Aveluy. On 28th July, after an early reveille, the Battalion entrained at the station close by, and made the journey north in those horse trucks so familiar to every soldier who served in France. Early next morning Arques (near St. Omer) was reached. A march of two miles brought it to the village of Campagne, around which, in scattered billets, the Battalion found a home for the next six weeks.

In this picturesque locality we had few idle moments. It was near this area that the Battalion had billeted on its arrival from Egypt, and Renescure and Roquetoire were accessible to those who had sufficient energy to visit them after having taken part in the long daily route marches.

Full packs were always carried, but a spice of novelty was added by the wearing of gas masks, causing an expectorating Battalion to trudge up the steep hill which lay between billets and parade ground.

Cookers at Martinpuich.

Many old friends were revisited, and new ones made, but the price of both eggs and champagne had soared far above the market rates of April, 1916.

The Canal leading to St. Omer was a popular and convenient swimming place, but sometimes the desire for a swim was whetted by a route march to a distant bathing hole. It was not all work; Paris leave became more general, and St. Omer was within convenient distance; there we saw, for the first time, the pleasant faces of the W.A.A.C.'s.

Brigadier-General J. Paton, C.B., C.M.G., who had succeeded General Gellibrand as Brigadier, met the Brigade for the first time at a Church Parade at Campagne, and there were two big inspections. The old hands were not slow in finding in these inspections the omens of impending stunts and hop-overs.

On 22nd August General Birdwood inspected the whole of the 2nd Division as it marched in column of route from Wardrecques to Campagne. The weather was showery, and detracted from what would otherwise have been a most impressive spectacle. The bands of various Battalions had a busy morning, and careered up and down the tow-path of the Canal, playing "details" past the saluting point.

On 29th August the Division formed up in mass for inspection by Field-Marshal Sir Douglas Haig. This was indeed a fine sight, and after the march past, the Field Marshal's favourable impressions were reflected in his very laudatory remarks.

The afternoon of 29th August was to have been devoted to aquatic sports, but inclement weather caused a postponement. They were successfully held before the area was quitted. The weather was very variable, and interfered considerably with the local harvesting operations. Members of the unit rendered much assistance to farmers in gathering in the crops, but were not impressed by the obsolete methods generally employed.

Tactical exercises did not play as prominent a part as at Beaulencourt, but there was one grand gathering when the Army Commander, General Plumer, attended to see the Brigade "capture" a wood. He expressed satisfaction, but there is little doubt that the unexpected appearance of numerous frightened hares put up by the attackers caused a certain amount of distraction.

At Campagne all ranks were frequently before the camera. Battalion Headquarters were in a chateau, the property of a French family, whose charming daughter photographed almost every individual in the Battalion.

On the evening of 2nd September enemy aircraft appeared over the village, and greatly perturbed the inhabitants. They were much more perturbed when it became known that the Battalion was to leave for the front line area. Our relations had been very cordial, and it was with mutual regret we parted, and on 12th September commenced our march once more towards the battlefield of Ypres.

CHAPTER XIII.

YPRES.—SEPTEMBER TO NOVEMBER, 1917.

Broodseinde.

When the Battalion moved from Campagne on 12th September, it marched via Ebblinghem to billets outside Steenvoorde, and the fact that not a man fell out during this long journey made in full marching order, justified the strenuous route marches of the preceding weeks.

One night in these billets and a couple of days in Dominion Camp preceded our entry into the line on the night of the 15th-16th September in a sector on Westhoek Ridge, taken over from the 17th and 19th London Regiments. Our Brigade held a double frontage, for the 5th and 7th Brigades were preparing for the attack of 20th September. We handed over to the former on the evening of the 18th-19th, and moved back by platoons to Ypres Asylum, which had been nominated as the Battalion rendezvous. Hot coffee and rum were there provided, and a happy meeting with a convoy of motor busses enabled the Battalion to make a speedy journey to Winnipeg Camp. Despite heavy shelling, much valuable preparatory and reconnaissance work had been done during the tour. The inevitable toll of casualties was, of course, incurred. Amongst the killed was Lieut. G. O. Greig, an officer whose connection with the Battalion dated back to Gallipoli days.

On 20th September (an exquisite summer day) the successful battle of Menin Road was fought, the Battalion being in reserve at Belgian Chateau, where an extraordinary aeroplane accident was witnessed, two of our machines colliding, and crashing with propellers locked together.

Next day the Brigade took over from the 5th and 7th Brigades the newly captured ground on the Becelaere Ridge, and on the night of the 21st-22nd September the Battalion relieved two battalions of the latter Brigade near Hannebeke Wood, in an area littered with German dead. Hostile shelling was heavy and continuous, and our casualties were numerous. "A" Company alone lost forty men during this tour of duty. Lieut. J. A. Thwaites was seriously wounded, and, in consequence, invalided to Australia.

The 13th Brigade relieved the 6th Brigade on 23rd September, and the Battalion moved back to Dominion Camp. German bombing planes were very active, and visited the area nightly. On two occasions we saw enemy machines caught in the concentrated rays of a dozen searchlights, and made target for the anti-aircraft and Lewis gun fire of the neighbourhood. Their escape only served to strengthen the general opinion as to the utility of anti-aircraft guns.

Throughout the whole Ypres fighting the aerial activity was remarkable; on occasions eighty and ninety machines might be seen in the air at one time. On 26th September the 4th and 5th Australian Divisions triumphed over the Hun at Polygon Wood. The Battalion at all times was in readiness to move up to the line on the shortest notice. Our Divisional Commander here carried out an inspection very early one morning. Inspections are never popular, but early morning visits are beyond comment, and there was general agreement among junior officers that when they attained seniority they would never subject a unit to the ordeal before midday.

From Dominion Camp the Battalion moved to the ruins of Ypres, and from there, on the night of 1st October, relieved two companies of the 34th Battalion, A.I.F., in the support line along Zonnebeke Ridge. Capt. W. S. G. Woolf was wounded during the relief, and was afterwards invalided to Australia; Lieut. W. McC. Braithwaite, M.C., thereupon took charge of "C" Company. "A" Company, under Captain W. H. Bunning, M.C., who were at Muhl, lost heavily on the afternoon of 2nd October from shell fire. That evening "B" and "D" Companies, under Captains H. C. Rodda, M.C., and E. A. Davis, M.C., respectively, relieved the 23rd Battalion in the front line near Zonnebeke Lake, and final orders were issued and preparations made for an attack on the morning of the 4th. The "J.O.T." for this was laid before midnight on 3rd October by the 6th Field Company. It ran about 100 yards in rear of our own outpost line, whose garrison withdrew to the "J.O.T." All night there had been drizzling rain, the morning was cold and raw, and the going naturally heavy.

The Battalion lined the "J.O.T." without incident in the following order of companies from left to right:—"A," "B," "C," and "D," and at 4 a.m. were lying in shell holes awaiting zero hour. This was fixed for 6 a.m. From 4 a.m. to 5.30 a.m. there was intermittent hostile shelling. At the latter hour every gun ceased, but the silence only lasted five minutes. At 5.35 a.m. a furious German barrage fell suddenly around the waiting men and on the evacuated line of outposts. It increased in intensity as our zero hour drew near, and the last ten minutes were very anxious ones for all, not least for those who occupied the shell holes. Each one felt that

Near Bellevarde Wood.

Some of the Boys at Westhoek.

surely he was the sole survivor, and there was mutual amazement and surprise when, at zero hour, as our own barrage crashed out, almost the entire body disengaged themselves from the debris and earth thrown over them by enemy shells, and pushed forward towards Broodseinde. Of the men reported "missing, 4th October," most met their death during the half hour which preceded the actual attack.

The morning was one of surprises. Our own barrage was the densest and best under which this Battalion has ever advanced, and, as was soon learned, caused consternation in the Hun ranks. His artillery ceased almost entirely, and the ambitious plans made by him for that morning were dramatically frustrated. He, too, had arranged an attack, with a zero hour coinciding with our own, and was on his "J.O.T." when our barrage fell. In the altered circumstances, he did not attempt a serious struggle, and prisoners surrendered freely. Almost without opposition the Battalion gained its objective—the "Red Line"—on the reverse slope of Broodseinde Ridge, and immediately commenced its consolidation, and the construction of a continuous trench system. The 21st and 24th Battalions waited on our objective until the barrage moved on with splendid accuracy, and enabled them to proceed to the second objective—the "Blue Line"—400 yards on the forward slope of Broodseinde Ridge. They accomplished their mission with great success, and the German Staffs who waited in "pill-boxes" for news of their own attack, had to accommodate themselves to quite a different situation.

One party of thirty, including a Colonel, his Staff, and several artillery liaison officers, surrendered to Pte. Drury, of "C" Company, when he entered their pill-box on exploration bent. They were formed up in file, and marched to the rear. The Adjutant, Capt. I. P. Stewart, M.C., in company with R. S. M. Cadwell, D.C.M., M.M., Croix de Guerre, picked up another party of twenty-five.

Battalion Headquarters moved forward to De Knoet Farm almost immediately the place was taken. The heavy shelling of the position they evacuated had not, of course, any connection with this speedy advance.

In one dugout in the vicinity of De Knoet Farm the occupants refused to surrender. Bombs had to be dropped through the ventilator, and next morning twenty-three corpses were removed.

Our casualties were comparatively light, but amongst the killed were Lieuts. R. Blanchard, F. G. Kellaway, M.C., and 2nd Lieut. J. McIntyre, who had all three served with the Battalion on Gallipoli, been promoted in the field, and fought at Pozieres. Lieut. Blanchard was one of the ill-fated thirteen who received their commissions during the battle of Pozieres.

The wounded included Major W. B. Craig, the well-known medical officer of the Battalion, who was so severely injured that he never rejoined again.

News of the success was sent to the rear by carrier pigeons. Two German pigeons were captured by another unit of the Brigade. The captors resisted the temptation to supplement their rations, and released one, to fly back to its German loft, with the attached message, "Deutschland uber Alles. Ha! Ha! We don't think."

The effect of our barrage was everywhere visible, and the peculiar circumstances connected with the attack caused the enemy extraordinarily high casualties.

Mention must be made of the part played by our machine gun barrage, which eclipsed even the German effort at Bullecourt.

The 1st Australian Division on our right, and 3rd Australian Division on our left, shared in the morning's victory, and made 4th October one of the most successful days in the history of the Australian Army. A large quantity of artillery maps and valuable documents were obtained by this Battalion, for the staffs captured had, in the expectation of a successful counter-attack, neglected to destroy their papers. Of more interest to the rank and file were the parcels which formed part of an undelivered German mail.

Two light guns had been brought forward by the Huns to cover their intended advance. Both were captured, one being undamaged. The undamaged gun was renamed "The Australian Hun Battery" and an officer detailed to work it against its previous owners. It was, of course, in a very forward and dangerous position, and to his obvious delight it was soon put out of action by a hostile 5.9.

The noise at night was terrific, as both sides maintained a fierce bombardment. As far as the eye could see, flares lighted the darkness, and S.O.S. signals (many unjustified) were too numerous to receive attention from the overworked artillery.

On the evening of 5th October the Battalion was relieved by the 20th Battalion, and went into reserve. Battalion Headquarters and "D" Company were at Hannabeke Wood, "C" Company at Muhl, and "A" and "B" Companies in the vicinity of Anzac House. The days which followed were most miserable, the weather was abominable, and regular downpours made the battle ground a quagmire.

The inevitable reaction after the battle of the 4th left all ranks thoroughly exhausted, but they could not be rested. The only accommodation consisted of shell holes, half filled with mud and water, and all available men worked long hours burying cables, and on the numerous fatigues

A relief was expected, for the men were completely worn out, but, instead, orders were received to move forward on the night of the 7th and relieve the 18th Battalion. Our fighting strength was now little more than 100, and it was necessary to bring up from Caestre the Battalion nucleus, that the line might be adequately held. Movement to the front line was through a communication trench, in parts waist deep in mud. Only those who went through the succeeding days can realise how miserable and depressing were the conditions. The Brigade was in the 2nd Army, whose offensive action was temporarily ended, but our sector was at the junction of the 2nd and 5th Armies; the latter were to attack on the morning of 9th October, the Brigade having to co-operate with their effort on its left. As on the 4th, the outpost line was vacated before zero, and a "J.O.T." lined in rear. When the barrage opened "C" and "D" Companies, who were on the Battalion's right, simply re-garrisoned their original posts. "A" and "B" Companies, on the left, moved forward against enemy strong posts. The supporting artillery had been unable to move their guns forward through the mud, and the barrage was not good. Enemy machine gun fire was heavy, and though the allotted posts were mopped up, there were others close by which maintained a continuous fire throughout the day. There was no communication to the rear, and German snipers took a heavy toll. Only a handful of weary men were left at nightfall, and those in rear had despaired of seeing these again.

Lieut. K. S. Anderson, who had taken part in the attack with "A" Company, was severely wounded, and during the next twenty-four hours endured extraordinary hardships, which only an astonishing perseverance, under awful conditions, enabled him to overcome.

Lieut. A. Skene-Smith, M.C., who had returned to the Battalion only a few days before, was killed on the morning of the 9th, while Lieut. N. H. Dooley was badly wounded, and later returned to Australia.

Prior to and during the 9th October fighting the Battalion cookers were at Sans Souci, in which forward position they had their stand by the duckboard track, and were an "Australian Comforts Fund" to men of our own and many other Battalions. That belonging to "B" Company here earned the right to carry a gold stripe, being well punctured by bursting shrapnel.

At 4 a.m. on 10th October the 49th Battalion, A.I.F., provided a relief, and took over the front line posts, allowing the survivors of the battered 22nd to move back to a position on Broodseinde, now well behind the firing line. At 7 p.m. the same night a further move was made, the worn out remnants of the Battalion making their way slowly back to wretched dugouts on the Ypres-Comines canal, near Ypres. The condition of the surviving officers and men from fatigue, hardship, and exhaustion was deplorable in the extreme, but hot meals and plenty of sleep soon worked wonders in setting them up again.

On 11th October the Battalion entrained at Ypres Station for Abeele, and marched to Steenvoorde to the billets previously occupied.

The Companies were now organised as three platoons, and the necessary refitting and specialist training proceeded with. There were sports meetings and concerts, and in a short time the recent trials became only an unpleasant memory.

The Q.M., Lieut. D. T. Miles, here received his well-earned Captaincy, and commissions were granted to C.S.M. E. J. Dundas and Sergts. R. I. Bourke, C. W. Hutton, F. Howell, and A. R. Barker. 2nd Lieut. J. Lennon rejoined with his commission from a Cadet Battalion.

The list of decorations for work at Ypres was also published. This included a D.S.O. for Major W. B. Craig, a Bar to his Military Cross for Capt. I. P. Stewart, M.C., and M.C.'s for Capts. Bunning, Davis and Rodda, and 2nd Lieut. J. Kohn. No. 989 Cpl. "Barney" Horan received a bar to the D.C.M., won by him on the Peninsula, and D.C.M.'s were awarded to No. 123 Sergt. E. R. Bregnezer, No. 4131 Sergt. W. C. Harris, No. 603 Sergt. L. G. A. Good, and No. 2347 Pte. J. C. McFarlane. There were also many Military Medal awards.

After a restful fortnight at Steenvoorde the Battalion marched, on 27th October, via Abeele to Dominion Camp, and next day to a poor camp at Dickebusch.

The first week of November was cold and cloudy, with sharp biting winds, and, though rain seldom fell, the days were dull and miserable. The 7th November brought occasional gleams of sunshine, also orders to move to Westhoek to relieve the 20th Battalion in the support line. The relief was carried out that night without incident.

There was intermittent shelling throughout the tour, but casualties were light. Appropriately enough, we were within a few hundred yards of Polygon Wood Racecourse, when a wire came through that "Westcourt" had won the Melbourne Cup.

On 10th November heavy rain fell, and flooded all the shelters, but next day the 8th West Yorks. relieved the Battalion, who spent one night at Dickebusch, and on the 12th marched to Wippenhoek. On the Vlamertinghe-Reninghelst Road General Birdwood inspected the Brigade as it marched past.

The Ypres fighting from September to November, 1917, cost the Australian Corps 1289 officers and 26,502 men, and, though the operations in which they fell were uniformly successful, the policy of "limited objectives" was then in vogue, and after each costly gained victory the Hun was able to repair his broken line before another attack developed.

The Ypres battlefields were dreadful places, which, fortunately, the Battalion was never to re-visit. Its line work during the winter which followed was on another sector.

CHAPTER XIV.

WINTER—NOVEMBER, 1917-MARCH, 1918.

The winter of 1917-18 was not nearly so trying as that of 1916-17 spent on the Somme. Not only was the weather milder, but the demands made on the men were far less exacting, and there were camps and bathing and other facilities, close to the line.

On the 18th November, 1917, the Battalion crossed the frontier and marched into a part of Belgium that was new to it. Its destination was a hut camp, which nestled close under the dominating and tree-clad height of Mount Kemmel, from whose summit a magnificent view of the Ypres battlefield could be obtained.

The village of Kemmel, which lay on the "line" side of the mount, was in ruins, but the hill itself had protected the little hamlet of Locre which lay beyond. Over three years of war had passed, leaving it unharmed, and the most confirmed pessimist could not, at this time, have imagined the situation which obtained during April, 1918, when the Huns not only captured the Mount itself, but held for a time the obliterated village of Locre and reduced to ruins our winter metropolis, Bailleul.

There is not a happier time to be chronicled in our history than that spent at Kemmel huts. Winter, with its short, dull days, was drawing on apace; but the huts were comfortable and warm: for the latter circumstance we were indebted to liberal supplies of coal procured from several carelessly guarded coal dumps in the neighbourhood. On one evening only were fires unpopular. On that occasion a Hun aeroplane dropped six bombs within a few yards of the camp. Several huts were slightly damaged, and much displaced earth fell on the officers' mess, which was filled at the time with officers awaiting the evening meal; but no one was injured. During the anxious few minutes some very undignified attitudes were assumed by some usually very dignified officers.

The only available sports-ground was the slope of the mount, but there was considerable enthusiasm for sport in all its branches. At football the Battalion was phenomenally unlucky, losing half a dozen games by less than a goal on each occasion. It was an unprofitable time for those who wagered on our teams. In the tug-of-war competition, "B"

Company were the winners. In a challenge match between officers and sergeants, the former were pulled almost off the small parade ground by the brawny N.C.O's. Every afternoon, too, there was an attendance worthy of the Horse Guards at Whitehall to watch the change over of the battalion guard. This was due to a keen competition in guard-mounting between the Companies. "D" Company were the winners.

While the Battalion was at Kemmel, Captains W. H. Bunning, M.C., and V. C. Alderson, M.C., left us to transfer to the Indian Army; Captain W. J. Cawthorn followed a month later. They carried with them the good wishes of all ranks.

It was at Kemmel that some industrious statistician was able to prove to the satisfaction of himself and the rest of the camp that throughout all our battles No. 13 platoon had enjoyed phenomenal good fortune and suffered far less losses than any other platoon in the Battalion. On the other hand, No. 16 platoon had been extremely unfortunate, both as regards men and officers. Of the statistician's own name and fate there is now no record, but it is, nevertheless, a fact that, though thirteen is reputed to be an unlucky number, there were always abnormally few fatal casualties in this platoon.

We expected to spend Christmas Day in the front line, so the Christmas dinners were held during the second week in December. Each Company had a dinner, and, though we were only a few kilometres from the line, the Kemmel Christmas festivities hold pride of place in this Battalion. Elaborate menu cards were provided, and though no expense was spared in the purchase of food, almost as much was owed to the efforts of a few hard-worked "salvagers" in each Company. The excellence of these dinners was much aided by a generous donation of £100 from Mrs. Craig, wife of Major W. B. Craig, D.S.O., our well-known medico.

The officers' Christmas dinner was held later at Kortepyp Camp, close to Ploegsteert. It was to this place we marched from Kemmel shortly before Christmas, expecting a speedy visit to the line. Instead, we remained a month, training or working on reserve lines every morning and giving the afternoons to sport. A very strong team from the Twenty-Fourth Battalion defeated us at football by the customary narrow margin. A large number of men were always engaged in salvaging operations, now for the military's enrichment instead of their own, and in the construction of intricate barbed-wire obstacles to stay the expected German offensive.

On Christmas Day there were more dinners, and the festivities were prolonged far into the night, especially in "C" Company's lines, where Pte. Monar and party convivially entertained their friends at a rum supper. No one was forgotten in the Christmas goodwill, even Lieut. H.

J. King and his coal-dump guard receiving a substantial Christmas-box of soap shortly after an unexpected early morning visit from the Colonel.

On 12th January, 1918, the Battalion moved to Romarin and thence to a system of dug-outs called The Catacombs, just behind the celebrated wood of Ploegsteert. These catacombs were an underground dug-out city consisting of great timbered drives and tunnels into the side of Hill 63. In galleries driven at right-angles off the main passages, long rows of wooden bunks were erected. The place was electrically lighted, and, though the atmosphere was a trifle stuffy, troops fresh from the line were very appreciative of the solid comfort of a good, dry bed. Some idea of the magnitude of the Catacombs may be gained from the fact that they could comfortably house of couple of thousand men.

About the middle of January the Battalion went into the front line round La Basseville, facing the town of Warneton, in a area with a very bad reputation, owing to the number and size of the "minnies" employed by the Hun.

Our officer's patrols, under Lieut. C. W. Hutton, M.C., and others, were very active under extremely bad conditions, capturing several prisoners in their uniformly successful brushes with the enemy. C.S.M. T. S. Carter, D.C.M., also accounted for several Huns. One of these was an officer from whose body very valuable maps were obtained.

It rained heavily and continuously during the third week in January, and front line posts and communication trenches were flooded. The tour of duty was performed under conditions the like of which the Battalion had not known since Flers and Ginchy.

When relieved, the Battalion rested for a week at Romarin, moving on 27th January to Shankhill huts near Neuve Eglise. Everyone was looking forward to a long-promised month near the coast, in the proximity of a large city, though previous experience had made sceptics of most. However, on 30th January, the Battalion entrained at Neuve Eglise for the "village" of Selles, about 20 kilometres from Boulogne. We detrained at Lottinghem in the early hours of the morning and marched six kilometres, to find no village, but widely scattered billets, to visit all of which entailed quite a route march. We remained at Selles till 6th March. It has been described by those who were comfortably billeted there as "a quiet, pretty restful place." Others not so fortunate have found other names for the area. Certainly, never since its arrival in France had the Battalion been so far from the firing line, and leave was obtainable to Boulogne, to which a motor lorry ran daily.

In a Brigade football competition, in which the Battalion secured second place, our team defeated the Sixth A.A.M.C., but again succumbed to the Twenty-Fourth Battalion. The final was a splendid game, played before a large crowd, and barracking was keen.

A "Divisional Platoon Competition" for shooting and bayonet fighting was won by No. 10 platoon of "C" Company, under Lieut. E. Gorman, M.C. This platoon first carried off the Brigade competition and then defeated the winning platoons of the other brigades, thus securing the championship of the Division. To this result the excellent Lewis gun work of L.-Cpl. L. Binns, M.M., and bar, materially contributed.

A miniature rifle range was constructed and musketry was made a special feature of the training, the final course being fired at Lottinghem, about five miles distant.

The month's rest ended on 5th March. At 2.30 a.m. on the 6th reveille sounded, and by 5 a.m. the Battalion was at Lottinghem, whence it entrained for Steenwerck. That night was spent once more in Kortepyp Camp, and next day a position was taken up in reserve near Ploegsteert and the Catacombs.

On 11th March front line work commenced. After the usual four days in the outposts, the Battalion was relieved by the Twenty-First Battalion, who, two nights afterwards, were raided by the Hun after a heavy minnenwerfer barrage. For the next eight days we were again in reserve, though working every night around the front line posts, which on 23rd March were again garrisoned by the Battalion.

The gigantic "minnies," with which we had previously made acquaintance, were even more active than formerly, and caused us a number of casualties.

Amongst the killed were 2nd-Lieut. C. L. A. Robbins and 2nd-Lieut. W. H. Parsons, M.M., Croix de Guerre. The former, who had just returned with his commission from an Officers' Cadet Battalion in England, lost his only brother at Pozieres with this Battalion. Lieut. Parsons died of wounds, which he bore very bravely. His chief consideration, as he was being carried from the line, was that the stretcher-bearers should not unduly distress themselves on his account.

Word had now reached us that a tremendous German offensive had been launched on the Somme, and that all the old battlefields so hardly won had, within a few days, fallen once more into enemy hands. It was common knowledge, in which the Hun apparently shared, that the Australian Corps would be shifted south immediately. On 31st March an English regiment, which had been in the Somme fighting, relieved the Battalion in the front line, and by dawn on 1st April the last platoon was in Shankhill Camp. Next day motor buses were boarded at Neuve

Eglise and the Battalion was carried to Berthen, about nine kilometres from Bailleul.

From the big hill outside Berthen a last view was obtainable of the Ypres and Flanders battlefields, with Zillebeke standing out most prominently.

During this move the first issue of the "Twenty-Second's Echo" was circulated. This little Battalion newspaper was greatly appreciated, and printed, as it was, on a small hand-press that accompanied the unit in dug-out and trench, it constituted something of a record in journalism. The paper was greatly appreciated from the outset, and appeared thenceforth every fortnight until the unit's demobilisation. Sergeant C. R. Blatchford was the Editor, and of all the difficulties and dangers attending the publication, he could tell many a good story. The circulation averaged about 600 copies, and at demobilisation the printing press was donated to the Australian War Museum.

On 4th April the Battalion reached the village of Godwaersvelde, where a train was waiting to convey it to the Somme once more.

CHAPTER XV.

"THE SOMME ONCE MORE."—APRIL-MAY, 1918.

Of the many weary, muddy, and often bloody days during which the Australian Corps sweated and fought on the Somme, none are of more glorious memory than those of 1918, when the victorious tide of German invasion was stemmed and Amiens saved by Australian Divisions.

In the Allied Nations an uneasy public marvelled at the strength and success of the Boche blow. In public, men boasted their confidence of the issue; in secret, they fought against a growing apprehension of what the future might hold.

Meantime the Australian Corps was adding to "that series of performances, unsurpassed in this great war" so generously recognised by the Fourth Army Commander, General Sir H. S. Rawlinson, in his well-known order:—

> "I feel that no mere words of mine can adequately express the renown that they have won for themselves, and the position they have established for the Australian Nation, not only in France, but throughout the world."

Who could resist quoting M. Clemenceau's classic of simple praise?

> "We knew you would do well: we did not know you would astonish a Continent."

With the Somme struggles and successes the Battalion had been intimately connected. In July, 1916, just prior to Pozieres, it had paid its first visit to Amiens, then a splendid and busy city. Battered, but victorious, the Regiment had quitted the Somme to "rest" in a quieter sector, and to repair the ravages of that dreadful battle. After a brief stay in the north, it had returned to know a Somme winter of unusual and intense severity. It had followed up the Hun during his retreat early in 1917, and with its sister Battalions had won great glory at Bullecourt, many miles from the Picardy capital.

The fluctuating fortunes of war had now enabled the Hun to overrun the old battlefields, capture Albert, and bring his forces to the very gates of Amiens. The city was under his fire, its splendid Cathedral in danger, its streets littered with debris and tangled wire. The morale of the Twenty-Second was magnificent, and every man was, at least temporarily, exalted by the emergency, and by his knowledge of the seriousness of the time.

News arrived that the Hun had captured the Warneton sector within forty-eight hours of our departure. At first few credited the story. Too many had worked on the intricate barbed-wire defences erected there throughout the winter by the Australian Corps to believe that the ground could possibly be lost.

When confirmation came, all vowed a new vengeance against the Hun. The "Town Major of La Basseville"—the usually placid Major Dooley—was moved to an unusual vehemence. He had for many days and nights, and at much personal risk, supervised the construction of defences there.

The pleasanter story of the initial Boche defeat sustained near Amiens at Australian hands cannot be told here. Our Third, Fourth, and Fifth Divisions had given the enemy his first reverse on this front. How our Battalion followed, as part of the Second Division, and continued the work will be narrated in the chapters following.

At 4 a.m. on 4th April, the Battalion entrained at Godwaersvelde, and at 6 a.m. on the 5th detrained at St. Roche station, Amiens. It was a dreary, misty morning. Amiens was deserted, except for a few scattered groups of civilians passing and making for the railway station.

The Kaiser and his staff regained no popularity in our unit during the trying eleven kilometre march to Bertangles, a village packed close with troops, where the night was spent.

Early next day the Battalion, now in fighting kit, was taken by 'bus to La Houssoye, on the main Albert-Amiens road, and after a march through Franvillers, halted at St. Lawrence Farm, where orders were received that it would that night relieve the combined Forty-Sixth and Forty-Seventh Australian Battalions and elements of others, in the front line near Dernancourt. These had been in much hard fighting during their tour of duty, and had repelled many hostile attacks.

It was an eventful night, pitch dark and stormy. By an unhappy chance, the Boche fired a "twin-green" flare—at that time our S.O.S. signal. Our guns promptly put down a barrage, to which the enemy artillery replied in kind. To this pleasant accompaniment the relief proceeded, and before dawn the Twenty-Second Battalion had taken over a large section of the front overlooking Albert, still watched over by the Leaning Virgin, which crowned the steeple of the wrecked Cathedral. The statue's days were numbered, as soon after our arrival it was shot down by Australian artillery—not by the Hun, as was generally reported at the time.

An enemy attack was expected daily, the weather was never good, and the outpost line was not overburdened with modern comforts. The "Defence Scheme" was definite. "There will be no withdrawal. Every bit of ground will be fought for." Casualties were fairly numerous, owing to shell fire and offensive patrolling.

On 14th April the Battalion was pleased to sub-let the property for four days to our friends of the Twenty-First, with whom, for the rest of the month, was carried out a system of reliefs alternating between the front line and the support trenches surrounding Lavieville.

The last day of the month eclipsed its predecessors, and provided twenty-four hours of a continuous downpour. The expected attack never came, but tension was high and the strain severe. Two reliefs of the nucleus personnel stationed at Berteaucourt, that "home away from home," did much to ameliorate the men's lot, but very little shelter was available, and there was a lot of digging and wiring to be done.

Owing to the Boche advance, there were no facilities for bathing or changing underclothing; something had to be done, and from the contents of linen-presses in adjacent deserted houses much feminine attire was drawn and pressed into useful service. Some startling and unconventional toilettes were to be seen.

The villages in the sector were deserted by their unfortunate inhabitants, and were being rapidly destroyed. Very little could be done to save even the abandoned portable property, and the sight of comfortable homes deserted and crumbling daily under shell-fire brought home very forcibly a realisation of what war meant to a civilian population.

The front line tours were marked by a number of patrol encounters, in one of which Lieut. A. R. Barker—an original member of the Battalion, and one of its prominent footballers—was killed. For his gallantry on this occasion Sgt. C. R. Waxman received the Military Medal. Lieut. J. H. B. Armstrong was wounded on another patrol, and 2nd-Lieut. J. M. Sutherland was wounded a few days later.

A skilful German sniper opposite the Battalion's right flank caused many casualties. He devoted his undoubted ability against our sergeants, six of whom he disabled before he himself was accounted for.

A feature of this sector was the constant strafing of Pioneer Trench and the Albert-Amiens road. The bombardments used to come in short violent bursts and would soon sever all signal wires running to the forward positions. It was in re-establishing communications on one of these occasions that Lieut. L. A. McCartin was wounded. His excellent work here was later recognised by the award of a Military Cross.

On 1st May the Battalion was relieved by the Twenty-First London

Battalion, and came out to Warloy, whence next morning the march was resumed through Contay, Beaucourt, Montigny, Behencourt, and Pont Noyelles, to Querrieu. The Brigade was here held in readiness to counter-attack, should the Huns break through, on the Villers Bretonneux front.

On 5th May General Sir W. R. Birdwood and General N. M. Smythe, V.C., were present at the Brigade church parade held in the picturesque grounds of Querrieu Chateau. The former addressed the troops and presented ribands and medals.

The main event during the week's rest was the celebration of the third anniversary of the Battalion's departure from Australia. Food and drink worthy of the occasion were obtained with great difficulty, but the results justified the trouble taken. After dinner a concert, arranged by the ever-ready L.-Cpl. Larry Herz, was received with enthusiasm by as many as could crowd into the semi-demolished barn which served as a threatre.

On 9th May the Battalion relieved the Thirty-Ninth Battalion, A.I.F., in the front line before Ville-sur-Ancre and Morlancourt. The country was now covered with luxuriant crops and clover, in the midst of which the enemy and ourselves had established outposts. Every night some portion of our line was pushed forward, by methods known to those not actually engaged in the operations as "peaceful penetration." It is difficult to imagine a greater misnomer. A number of prisoners were taken, and Lieut. H. M. M. Wall distinguished himself greatly in patrol work, for which he was awarded a Military Cross.

In the neighbouring village of Treux the R.S.M., while on a tour of exploration, found an emaciated young kid, aged about three weeks. This little goat was adopted by the Transport Section, and, after being bottle-fed, thrived wonderfully. "Bill" accompanied the Battalion in all its subsequent wanderings along the front, and made numerous appearances before the Official Photographer.

The Hun was now showing great activity with gas-shells and machine-guns, and on 13th May attacked the Fifth Brigade, who were on our immediate right, only to receive a crushing defeat. Practically the whole of the attacking force were killed or taken prisoners.

It was now common gossip that the Brigade was shortly to "relieve the Hun" at Ville-sur-Ancre, and that to this Battalion had been allotted the major share in the attack.

The persistency with which rumours of an impending "stunt" were circulated was sometimes annoying to the Higher Command, who were interested in maintaining secrecy. Not less remarkable was the almost invariable accuracy of the predictions.

As a preliminary to the attack, the Battalion was relieved on the night of 14th May by the Twenty-First Battalion, and went into support at Ribemont.

Seldom has the morale been better on the eve of a "stunt." The 16th May was a glorious day, and everyone was in high spirits as they read, played, or slept in the sun.

On the night of 17th-18th May, the J.O.T. was pegged out by the Engineers, assisted by Lieut. E. Thewlis, in readiness for the attack, which was to be made twenty-four hours later.

CHAPTER XVI.

VILLE-SUR-ANCRE.—MAY, 1918.

How critical this period was will probably never be realised by any but a few; how great the work of the Australian Corps appears from the official figures disclosing the numbers of prisoners and guns captured by them during the fateful months of April, May, and June, 1918.

It must be remembered that these months were quiet, stagnant ones on the British front and that, while most of the Army was recovering from the hard fighting of March, the Australians alone were on the offensive—not an offensive of grand attacks and large advances, but a series of nibbles, raids, and local operations, carried out with a daring and stealthiness that unnerved the opposing enemy divisions. The success of these "bush tactics" (as one German general described them) may be gauged from the fact that 85 officers, 3700 men, 38 trench-mortars, and 400 machine-guns were, during this period, captured by the A.I.F. alone. A letter captured from a Hun in one of our raids about this time mentioned a dread of the Australians, "who creep up to our posts at night like cats, killing and carrying off."

The Twenty-Second Battalion took no small part in this novel warfare, and the Australian Corps for nearly four months sustained, unaided, its offensive work, while the rest of the British Army re-organised and prepared its defences.

The last chapter brought us to the eve of one of the most decisive and earliest successes of this time and one which was, more than any other, a Twenty-Second Battalion battle, as this unit was the only complete Battalion in the Ville-sur-Ancre attack, and supplied the bulk of the troops engaged. This village was essential to the Boche for the defence of Morlancourt and was the first important village to be regained by the Allies after the Hun offensive, the capture of Villers-Bretonneux (where the Fifth Australian Division had so distinguished itself) taking place during the period of the Boche offensive itself.

Some Ville-sur-Ancre Trophies.

Some Old Originals.

At the time the importance of the Ville-sur-Ancre victory in raising British morale and contributing to the destruction of those high hopes inspired in the Boche by his earlier successes was universally recognised.

The plan adopted for the operation was to attack and seize the high ground to the south of the village and so force the enemy to evacuate.

This task was allotted to the Twenty-Second, the attack covering a frontage of three-quarters of a mile and penetrating to the same depth. The village itself was to be cleared and consolidated by companies of the Twenty-First and Twenty-Third Battalions.

The objective included two sunken roads, generally known as the "Big Caterpillar" and the "Little Caterpillar," strongly held by the enemy and guarded by a series of outposts, manned by machine-gunners. After capturing these objectives the Battalion was to link up with a company of the Twenty-Fourth Battalion east of the village, and thus allow parties of the two other sister Battalions to mop it up.

Shortly after midnight on 18th-19th May all four of our Companies were in position ready to attack, in the following order from left to right: "B," "A," "C," "D." Never before had the Battalion attacked over so large a frontage with so few men, from fifteen to twenty yards separating each man from his neighbour in the same wave on the "J.O.T."

Earlier in the evening, as "A" Company were moving into position, they had suffered fifteen casualties from a single shell.

Zero was fixed at the unusually early hour of 2 a.m., when an intense creeping barrage fell on the German lines. The attackers followed so closely upon it that they effectively surprised and captured the occupants of the enemy outpost line, who were not able, for the most part, to offer a desperate resistance.

On the outskirts of Ville-sur-Ancre and opposite the Battalion's left flank were a cemetery and a crucifix, both strongly held. These were attacked and captured at once, along with several machine-guns, by a party under Lieut. N. J. Madden.

In the "Big Caterpillar" heavy hand-to-hand fighting took place. The attackers were, as has been told, even originally, very few for the large Battalion frontage, and, by the time the "Big Caterpillar" was reached, there had been heavy casualties. The defenders were numerous and capable of a strenuous resistance. The intrepidity of 2nd-Lieut. (then Sergeant) W. Ruthven solved a most serious problem, and his signal bravery and determination earned for him the Victoria Cross. His feat is best described in the language of the "Gazette":—

"For most conspicuous bravery and initiative in action at Ville-sur-Ancre.

"During the advance Sgt. Ruthven's Company suffered numerous casualties and his Company Commander was severely wounded. He thereupon assumed command of this portion of the assault, took charge of the Company headquarters, and rallied the section in his vicinity.

"As the leading wave approached its objective, it was subjected to heavy fire from an enemy machine gun at close range. Without hesitation he at once sprang out, threw a bomb, which landed beside the post, and rushed the position, bayoneting one of the crew and capturing the gun. He then encountered some of the enemy coming out of the shelter. He wounded two, captured six in the same position, and handed them over to an escort from the leading wave which had now reached the objective.

"Sgt. Ruthven then reorganised the men in his vicinity, and established a post in the second objective.

"Observing enemy movement in a sunken road near by, he, without hesitation, and armed only with a revolver, went over to the open alone and rushed the position, shooting two enemy who refused to come out of their dug-outs. He then single-handed mopped up this post and captured the whole of the garrison, amounting in all to 32, and kept them until assistance arrived to escort them back to our lines.

"During the remainder of the day this gallant non-commissioned officer set a splendid example of leadership, moving up and down the position under fire, supervising consolidation and encouraging the men. Throughout the whole operation he showed the most magnificent courage and determination, inspiring every one by his fine fighting spirit, his remarkable courage, and his dashing action."

This was the first Victoria Cross awarded to any member of the Sixth Brigade, and, when shortly afterwards 2nd-Lieut. Ruthven returned to Australia, he received a fitting welcome.

Within half an hour of Zero, success signals could be observed from all objectives except those on the extreme left flank, where, for a time, "B" Company could not go forward to their final objective, owing to portion of the barrage falling short. This short firing accounted, too, for a number of our own casualties. When it ceased, the company advanced, and the whole Battalion dug in on the crest of the slope overlooking Morlancourt. From this very advantageous position much "peaceful penetration" was proceeded with. Over two hundred prisoners and many machine-guns were captured by the Battalion during the morning.

The other Battalions engaged had also done splendidly, both in and beyond the village, and the total prisoners taken by the Brigade exceeded three hundred. This number was substantially added to by the complete success of the operations undertaken on our right by the Fifth A.I.F. Brigade.

The feature of the day, after the turmoil of the morning, was the almost entire absence of hostile rifle or artillery fire, with the exception of a few shells which fell late in the afternoon after a reconnaissance by a low-flying Boche plane.

Our own casualties were heavy, having regard to the numbers engaged; but the deaths were, fortunately, few.

Lieut. C. M. Bowden, who had joined the Battalion from an O.T.C., only a fortnight before, was killed, and Major J. S. Dooley, M.C., Capt. W. R. Hunter, Lieuts. N. C. Southwell, R. J. Bourke, W. M. Green, D.C.M., N. J. Madden, C. J. Fulton, and H. M. Wall were wounded, the firstnamed four being incapacitated from further service in France.

The decorations awarded included a D.S.O. for Major L. W. Matthews, M.C.'s for Lieuts. H. M. Wall, N. J. Madden, P. J. Abercrombie, C. W. Hutton, E. E. Patterson, and J. P. Greene, and D.C.M.'s for R.S.M. Cadwell, C.S.M.'s T. Carter and R. Werrett, and No. 3914, Sgt. F. G. Robinson. Nos. 117, Cpl. L. T. Binns; 160, Cpl. T. Gorman, and 2493, Sgt. R. E. Batton, each received bars to their Military Medals. Among the military medallists was Sgt. C. R. Blatchford, editor of the "Twenty-Second's Echo," who voluntarily relinquished his editorial duties for a few days in order to take part in the attack.

So successful was the entire operation and so important was it to the Higher Command, that on the following day General Birdwood visited Battalion Headquarters in the line to convey personally his thanks and appreciation.

About 11.30 p.m. on 20th May the Battalion was relieved in the front line by the Twenty-Eighth Battalion, portion of whom had acted as carrying parties during the operations, and moved back to Franvillers. The Battalion Band played the victors home along the Amiens-Albert road, and for some hours after the main body had passed stragglers could be seen jealously guarding the captured trophies they were dragging from the battlefield.

The ten days which elapsed before the Battalion's next visit to the line were spent at Franvillers, to which Hun artillery was now paying such unwelcome attention that the village could no longer be used, and the Battalion "dug in" in trenches on the outskirts. The services of the Official Photographer were now secured for a few days and a large number of photos taken for official records and with a view to their insertion in this history.

The Ville-sur-Ancre trophies were at the same time despatched to the Australian War Museums. Most of the men were required every night for fatigue parties, and only a few were available for "specialist training."

CHAPTER XVII.

TO VILLERS-BRETONNEUX.—MAY-AUGUST, 1918.

The short stay at Franvillers soon came to an end, but the excellent weather, combined with fairly pleasant surroundings, had put all ranks in the best of form for further work in the line.

The move forward was made on 31st May, and that night the Battalion relieved the Twenty-Eighth Battalion in front of Mericourt, occupying the support lines known as Treux, Ballarat, and Bendigo trenches. The weather continued good and work remained plentiful, as there was no cessation of the nightly digging parties. On one of these an extraordinary accident happened. While digging a trench there was unearthed the body of a dead soldier, in whose pocket was a bomb. A pick unfortunately penetrated the clothing and either withdrew the pin or, in some other manner, exploded the bomb, which killed Sgt. E. A. Smith (a Gallipoli veteran) and wounded Lieut. W. McC. Braithwaite, M.C.

On 7th June the Battalion replaced the Twenty-First in the firing line and commenced an eight-day tour of duty, during which Lieut. John Lennon was killed. On the afternoon of his death he executed alone, and on his own initiative, a daylight raid on a German post, securing valuable information and some identifications from enemy dead. The same night Lieut. Lennon led a patrol against the same post and brought back several prisoners. Unfortunately, he was killed by a machine-gun bullet when re-entering our lines.

On 10th June, before dark, a party in charge of Lieut. L. W. Harricks, under a heavy barrage of high-explosive and smoke-shell, raided the Hun line with complete success, killing thirty Huns and capturing six prisoners and a machine-gun, without suffering a single casualty. For this dashing operation Lieut. Harricks received the Military Cross, and a number of the raiders were also decorated.

On 15th June the sector was handed over to the Fifty-Ninth Bat-

Lieut. W. Ruthven, V.C.

talion, and the Twenty-Second established itself under trench shelters in the La Houssoye system, between Querrieu and the village from which the trenches took their name, and within sight of the memorial erected to the French soldiers who fell in 1870 during a battle in the neighbourhood.

Both villages were at this time receiving a good deal of artillery fire, but this did not prevent frequent cricket matches in the chateau grounds, where, also, a Battalion Sports Meeting was held, "C" Company winning the championship.

On 23rd June the Battalion had its first inspection by the new Corps Commander, General Sir John Monash, when he presented decorations and ribands, and in a stirring speech outlined the heavy work yet to be done.

The other main incidents of this time were the good news from Italy, Hun aeroplane activity by night, and the arrival of "Spanish Influenza."

The move of the Battalion into the famous Villers-Bretonneux sector was now imminent. On 28th June a march was made to Glisy, and divisional reserve trenches occupied near the village. Many a man will go to his grave firmly persuaded that the Twenty-Second Battalion has done more digging and buried more signal cables than any other unit in France. This arduous and fatiguing work (now nightly undertaken) became tiresome in the extreme, but everyone showed the right spirit in getting the work done first and leaving the growling until afterwards.

On 2nd July the Hon. W. M. Hughes and Sir Joseph Cook, accompanied by the Corps and Divisional Commanders, inspected a special parade at Lamotte and addressed the troops. That night the Battalion relieved the Twentieth Battalion in reserve close to the front line.

On 4th July the victory of Hamel was gained and 1500 prisoners taken by the Australian Corps, but owing to its losses at Ville-sur-Ancre and depleted strength, this Battalion did not take part in the actual attack. However, excellent work was done by the thirty officers and one hundred men of the unit, who, under heavy fire, and with twenty casualties, dug a communication trench from the old front line to the newly captured positions. A few days after the Hamel fight the Battalion moved again; this time to the "famous" Aubigny system. Our ability at and affection for cable burying had now apparently received a wide notoriety, for on 10th July the Battalion was attached to the Seventh Brigade for this purpose.

It was the Hun who provided a diversion.

At 11.30 p.m. on 16th July he commenced a barrage of the Aubigny system and neighbouring area with gas-shells. Between that hour and 2.30 a.m. on the 17th he threw over 7000 shells, completely saturating the area with mustard-gas. A heavy thunderstorm was followed by a bright, sunny day, and, although box-respirators were worn for hours and the immediate locality evacuated, the gas hung about for days and two hundred casualties resulted, a number of which proved fatal.

Our strength was now so reduced that "A" and "B" Companies had to be amalgamated temporarily, and the authorities were unable to build up the strength for the time being, owing to the slump in enlistments at home.

On 19th July the Battalion relieved the Twenty-Fifth Battalion in the firing line, east of Villers-Bretonneux. By day the line was quiet, but at night there was much machine-gun fire, and the flatness of the country made indirect fire dangerous, even at a considerable distance from the line, for at night all movement was overland.

On 22nd July the Hun put on Villers-Bretonneux a barrage of gas-shells even more intense than that from which we had suffered in the Aubigny system. When the barrage opened there were many ration-carrying parties en route for the scene of their labours, for, though holding the outpost line very lightly, the slender garrisons in the isolated posts had to be weakened every night for the conveyance of rations from a considerable distance.

From 10 p.m. on 22nd till early morning on 23rd July thousands of yellow-cross gas-shells fell in the ruins and the gas was blown back over the ration dumps and the Battalion Headquarters. It was only by elaborate precautions that the casualties were confined to about fifty. The other Battalions in the Brigade and all units in the vicinity suffered much more heavily. At this time most of the other casualties resulted from machine-gun fire, though every afternoon the left company sector was intensely bombarded. It was a stray bullet which killed Lieut. R. Swanton at his post in the outpost line one evening during this tour.

On 27th July the Battalion was associated for the first time with the Americans. On that date "K" Company of the Third Battalion, One Hundred and Twenty-Ninth American Regiment was attached to the Twenty-Second Battalion for experience. One American platoon was allotted to each of our three companies and one was kept in support. This one full-strength American Company considerably outnumbered our entire Battalion. Very ardent soldiers they were and their admiration for our men and deference to their judgment was almost embarrassing. The Battalion remained in the line till 29th July, when the Twenty-First

Battalion took over, and, with our American companions, we provided company garrisons for the "keeps" of Villers-Bretonneux. Not to rob the Americans of the desired "experience," the Battalion resumed its nocturnal role of cable-laying and introduced them to its joys.

The heavy nature of the manual labour performed so continuously, the strain of living so long in the forward area, and the two gas attacks had left their effects on the men. Everyone thought a corps relief must soon come or that a divisional relief at least was certain. These anticipations were greatly at fault, for the events of the preceding months were but a prelude to others of much greater magnitude in which the whole Corps was to take part immediately.

On August 2nd the Twenty-Eighth Battalion took over the Battalion's positions west of Villers-Bretonneux, and we moved to closer support east of that town. On the 5th the Americans were withdrawn and there were vague rumours of a gigantic "stunt." Some days previously an interesting memo. had been circulated, in the interests of concealing intentions, urging all ranks, under threat of "disciplinary action," to use the communication trenches in rear of the outpost line instead of walking overland. The purpose was obvious, but these trenches were very wet and very muddy, and it was interesting to note the struggle between "dry feet and duty" when immaculately-dressed senior officers had occasion to move round the area. It is regrettable to have to state that duty rarely triumphed.

On 7th August, when final arrangements for the great attack were completed, the Battalion was holding the outpost line. Late in the afternoon of that day a great fire commenced in Villers-Bretonneux. It subsequently transpired that about a dozen supply tanks had been burnt, through an enemy shell landing amongst them. It was now definitely announced that the projected attack would be launched on 8th August, and a special Order of the Day was issued for circulation to all ranks, which dwelt upon the importance of the operations and their probable far-reaching consequences. Three hours before zero on the morning of 8th August the Battalion evacuated the outpost line, leaving only a few posts of one officer and ten men each. These kept an anxious watch until just before dawn, when they, too, withdrew. Our guns then put down a smothering and demoralising barrage, and the great victorious attack of 8th August, 1918, was soon in full swing.

CHAPTER XVIII.

VILLERS-BRETONNEUX AND HERLEVILLE.—AUGUST, 1918.

During the concluding days of July, 1918, the German offensive spirit definitely collapsed. The last grand attack of 15th July against the French front had, thanks to a masterly counter-stroke, ended in disaster. The dramatic Australian and Canadian victory at Amiens, foreshadowed in the last chapter, was speedily to follow.

Much has been written of "accumulated reserves" which rendered the Amiens victory possible, but it was the Australians Corps, "the backbone of the defence," who were, with the Canadians, to act now as "the spear-head of the attack." The only other British infantry engaged on 8th August were two English divisions on the extreme left flank. Strict secrecy had been kept until the days immediately preceding the attack and the assembly of tanks and cavalry had been postponed until the last possible moment. In perfect conception and masterly execution, the operations were unique and the almost mechanical accuracy with which provision had been made for every detail by the Australian Staff begot a spirit of confidence in speedy final victory such as had never previously existed.

The general plan was to strike on an eleven-mile frontage in an easterly and south-easterly direction, with the Somme River as a protection for the left flank, releasing Amiens and the Amiens-Paris railway, subsequent developments depending on the measure of the initial success. This was actually so brilliant as to permit of the crowning triumphs of the next three months. There was a heavy ground mist when the barrage opened at 4.20 a.m. This helped in the early stages to conceal movement to the "J.O.T.," but later added to the difficulty of maintaining direction. Only a few hostile batteries ever got into action; most of them were obliterated by the barrage, while the tanks, cavalry, and armoured cars disposed of any that survived it. Thirty minutes before schedule time the appointed Australian battalions were on the furthest day's objectives, six miles from the "J.O.T." The Canadians had also done magnificently,

Some Well-known Characters.

Officers, September, 1917.

and the attached tanks, cavalry, and motor machine-gun brigades overran all opposition.

As a spectacle, the scene, when the ground mist lifted, surpassed anything men had seen in four years of war. Along the Warfusee-Amiens road, the main communication, an ordered mass of infantry, artillery, and every form of transport moved rapidly forward and not a single enemy gun remained in action to play upon the congestion. In the distance large bodies of cavalry could be seen, with none to bar their way, and though everywhere there were targets, the hostile artillery was silent. On the captured guns thoughtful men were soon marking with material they had somehow obtained, "Captured by the —— Battalion, A.I.F." Sometimes one, more thoughtful than they, would bring paint and obliterate the number of the first marked battalion by painting over it that of his own.

Following the Fifth Brigade, the Twenty-Second Battalion moved forward into what had, earlier in the morning, been the German front line. Next day it advanced in artillery formation to Guillacourt, where an enormous German dump sheltered all the companies. August 10th was a beautiful day, free from enemy shelling, and the Battalion held carnival; the band was brought up to play sweet music; the giant railway gun captured by the Eighth A.I.F. Brigade was near by and all day attracted crowds of sightseers; and there were even fireworks at night. These were obtained from the dozens of multi-coloured flares abandoned by the enemy, but the unauthorised illuminations soon came under an official ban.

The following evening the Sixth Brigade took over part of the firing line, the Twenty-Second Battalion relieving portions of the Nineteenth and Twenty-Eighth Battalions. Battalion Headquarters at Framerville were, for a time, in a cellar, small, thinly roofed, and lying in an area continuously shelled by guns of heavy calibre. At the entrance was a pile of malodorous dead horses still harnessed to limbers as they had been shot by the armoured cars on 8th August. A speedy change was effected to an old Boche dug-out in the ravine east of the village, much nearer the line, but further from the horses. Framerville and the neighbouring village of Rainecourt contained many interesting German documents; the former possessed even a well-stocked book store. The next few nights were busy ones, for each evening the line was advanced from three hundred to five hundred yards by "peaceful penetration." The ground was entirely free from trenches or cover, and after each "penetration" new trenches had to be dug before dawn. The Battalion mustered only one hundred and thirty rifles, and as the front line posts had also to carry up their own rations, each man was called on to do the work of three. Everyone good-humouredly responded to every demand made, but the strain was none the less great. All were soon to be tried even more sorely. By 17th August the line had been pushed to within about four hundred yards of strong German posts on the outskirts of the village of Herleville. These were garrisoned, as was later ascertained, by portion of a Guard Division specially brought from reserve with instructions to stay at all costs any attack that might be attempted. They were supported by strongly reinforced artillery, which was always active, its fire rising frequently to barrage intensity.

The Twenty-Fourth, Twenty-Second, and Twenty-Third Battalions held the Brigade frontage in that order from left to right. Between the two first-named was a road which led into Herleville, and a few hundred yards to the right of the village and about four hundred yards in front of our posts was a crucifix. Village and crucifix were connected by a sunken road, traversed in places by trenches and bordered on the far side by a high bank, which served as a parapet for a strongly held trench. Around the crucifix itself there was a simple trench system. On 17th August orders were received for an attack at 4.15 a.m. on the 18th. The Twenty-Second Battalion were to occupy the sunken road and at the same time the Twenty-Fourth Battalion were to advance the right half of their line. Their right and the Twenty-Second's left flank were to rest on the dividing road previously mentioned, and the Twenty-Second and Twenty-Third Battalions were to junction four hundred yards to the right of the crucifix. The additional ground to be gained by this operation was of no particular value and the tired men were in numbers pitifully few for the frontage allotted. These facts were most strongly and fully represented, but, nevertheless, definite orders were received to carry out the attack, and all preparations were at once made. So depleted was the Battalion's fighting strength that only with difficulty could a total of one hundred and twenty bayonets be raised. Of these, "C" Company (thirty all ranks) had to be retained as support in the front line and the remaining ninety men were faced with the task of assaulting the German line on a front of over half a mile. Wave formations were obviously impracticable and thin section groups were formed for the attack.

Owing to the limited artillery available, the barrage was arranged in "lanes" only on selected places, and, in point of fact, this did not prove effective.

"B" Company were on the left, "A" Company in the centre, and "D" Company on the right. The attack was met by heavy artillery and machine-gun fire from the outset, but "D" Company captured their objective. Advancing over open country, this Company lost twelve men of its original thirty before reaching it, but the survivors of the eighteen who got there held on till assistance arrived later in the morning and successfully consolidated one-half of the objective allotted to the Battalion.

Lieut. Leo McCartin, M.C., commanded this Company. He had with him Lieut. N. J. Madden, M.C., and Lieut. L. Speak. Lieut. Madden was killed by a shell while crossing "No Man's Land" at the head of his little party.

Lieut. McCartin was twice wounded early in the attack, but continued on to the objective. When he found the crucifix on his left still strongly held by the enemy, he made his way across the open and past this strong post to the headquarters of the support company, whence telephonic communication was maintained with Battalion Headquarters. He was again seriously wounded; this time in the face, but, saying nothing of his wounds, he outlined the position to the Colonel and requested instructions.

At this stage Lieut. W. Braithwaite, M.C., who commanded the support company, took the telephone and acquainted the Colonel with the seriousness of McCartin's condition and that he was too seriously wounded to carry on. The latter was immediately ordered to the rear. He laughingly acknowledged the order and left the trench, but, instead of making his way out, tried, to rejoin his men on their objective, and was killed in the attempt. This very gallant and most popular officer left Australia as a private with the Battalion, and will be always held in affectionate memory by all with whom he was brought in contact.

"A" Company, in the centre, had been faring badly. They were only twenty-four all told, but in five small sections, at about seventy yards intervals, they reached the sunken road and commenced a bombing fight with the Germans in the trench beyond. Lieuts. C. J. Fulton and J. Evans were both wounded and the command fell to Lieut. Harold Smith, M.M. It was not until ten of the twenty-four had been killed or wounded and no more bombs were left that the impossible was abandoned, and the little party withdrew to a communication trench by the crucifix. Later they succeeded in establishing themselves on the right flank of their objective. Amongst the killed of this company was Sgt. Ellis. To the last he set a magnificent example to his men, urging them on, throwing bombs, and fighting desperately till his end came.

In the midst of this desperate fight there was one almost humorous incident. A party working up a communication trench towards the crucifix killed three Germans, but a fourth escaped into the sunken road and ran along it. He was seen by Pte. Holloway, M.M., who, forgetful of all else, jumped into the road and chased the fugitive, regardless of enemy fire. After a stern chase, he got sufficiently close to his quarry to "harpoon" him with his bayonet, and then made his way back into safety.

Of the many brave deeds performed that morning, none excelled that of Lieut. S. Woods, of the Seventh Machine Gun Company. He was attached to "A" Company and had volunteered for the duty. When he saw this Company in difficulties, he rushed forward and established his gun on a mound in full view of the enemy and in the midst of bursting bombs. There he himself worked the gun, assisted by a battalion Lewis gunner who went to his aid. For a time, in miraculous fashion, he escaped injury, but an enemy bomb at last fell close by. In attempting to throw it back it burst in his hand, inflicting wounds from which he subsequently died in a Casualty Clearing Station.

On the extreme left, "B" Company suffered severely. Under the command of Lieut. H. W. Westaway, who had with him Lieuts. B. Armstrong and H. W. Mallinson, they set out, thirty-three strong, through heavy artillery and machine-gun fire. Most of them became casualties before reaching their objective, but those who arrived there joined forces in a large shell-hole within fifty yards of the enemy and opened fire with a Lewis gun and rifle grenades. The gun was soon knocked out of action by a bomb and the grenades expended. Sgt. Bregenzer, D.C.M., who had seen much heavy fighting with the Battalion, then tried to retrieve the situation by jumping into the open and calling on the Huns to surrender, but he was killed immediately. Neither the flares nor the S.O.S. signal sent up for artillery support were responded to, and the enemy worked closer, firing a machine gun and grenades into the now defenceless garrison of the shell-hole. Lieut. Westaway and several men were killed and most of the others were wounded before being surrounded by the enemy. The Twenty-Fourth Battalion party on this company's left suffered a similar fate, the survivors being also surrounded. From the crucifix to the left flank the attack did not succeed, not because of any lack of gallantry, but because no men, however gallant, could have succeeded. The attackers there did more than could reasonably be asked of any men, though their task was hopeless from the outset and, what is more, though many of them knew that it was so.

The manner in which Lieut. McCartin, Sgts. Bregenzer and Ellis, and many unnamed heroes sacrificed their lives in a forlorn hope was worthy of the glorious Battalion traditions they had themselves done so much to establish.

Le Sars.

Of the ninety men who took part in the attack, sixty were killed, wounded, or missing, and of these sixty, seven were officers.

All that was left of the Battalion, some seventy fighting men in all, was relieved the same evening by a Battalion of Yorkshire Light Infantry six hundred and seventy strong. Next morning the Germans delivered an attack and captured the front-line system, from which they were later dislodged by a strong counter-attack. These Germans were in every way superior to their ordinary infantry, for not only did they abstain from "ratting" the prisoners they had taken, but they also buried a number of our dead and erected a cross on their grave.

After the relief the remnants of the Battalion embussed for Vecquemont and thence marched to bivouacs, reached on the morning of 19th August. It was thought that a long rest from the line was now certain, but a church parade near Daours on the morning of 25th August was disturbed by orders to move forward at once.

The Battalion's continued existence as a fighting unit was made possible by the arrival at Vecquemont of a good body of reinforcements, dubbed the "New York Anzacs," because they had represented Australia at New York when passing through that city on the voyage over. That they were equally capable of representing Australia on the battlefield was proved in the fighting in which the Battalion was yet to participate.

NOTE.—It must be understood that there is a great difference between the *nominal* strength of a battalion and its *fighting* strength. The non-combatant portion of a battalion includes the Transport Section, Band, Q.M. Staff, Orderly Room Clerks, men on leave, and other details. In the Twenty-Second on this occasion these latter totalled some one hundred and eighty, which, added to the seventy fighting men, made the nominal strength about two hundred and fifty. In the case of the English Battalion mentioned as relieving us the nominal strength was over 1100, but the fighting strength was only six hundred and seventy.

CHAPTER XIX.

CAPPY AND MONT ST. QUENTIN—AUGUST-SEPTEMBER, 1918

Nearing Victory.

The few days' rest on the banks of the Somme at Vecquemont enabled the Battalion to be re-equipped, reinforced, and re-organised. A long spell could not be expected, as attack after attack was being made on the Hun, and the large daily advances showed that the tide of war was now set in our favour.

On 25th August, the Battalion left Vecquemont in motor busses, and, after a wet ride, debussed near some newly dug reserve trenches about four miles from the firing line. The next evening the Battalion relieved the Tenth and Eleventh Australian Battalions in freshly captured positions just beyond the ruined village of Cappy. The enemy was fighting a rear-guard action, depending mainly on isolated marchine-gun posts established in some of the old trenches which abounded in the area. The stoutness of the resistance offered by these rear-guards varied; sometimes they fought valiantly, at others not so well, but the days and nights of our advance parties were crammed full of excitement, for it was impossible to know which of the numerous trenches were occupied, and there was little time for careful scouting. Their duty was to locate and overcome enemy garrisons wherever found, whereupon they would notify Battalion Headquarters, and our front line and supports would then move forward. This constant advancing was terribly fatiguing, as sleep was a luxury, and the nerve strain was constant.

The relief was not complete until 2 a.m. on 27th August, but fighting patrols at once went forward in the darkness, engaging the enemy wherever found, with bomb and bayonet. By dawn, the firing line had been advanced 1500 yards, at the cost of some twenty casualties, of whom seven were killed in hand-to-hand fighting in the dark. Amongst those killed was Lieut. H. M. M. Wall, M.C., who, after being wounded in the Sixth Battalion at Anzac, had returned from Australia with reinforcements to this Battalion, and had soon won a high place in general esteem.

After hasty re-organisation at daybreak, the advance was continued until noon, the Twenty-Fourth Battalion passing through Dompierre with us, and mopping up the village. Our Lewis gunners here intercepted an attempt to withdraw two German field-guns, and shot the teams. The crews managed to damage the muzzles with explosives before making off, but left the guns to be withdrawn by our transport mules the same night, and eventually to be added to our exhibits in the Australian War Museum.

A further advance of 2000 yards was made on 28th August, when Black Wood, on the outskirts of Herbecourt, was reached. During the day an advance party of twelve, under Lieut. L. G. A. Good, D.C.M., were vigorously attacked by a number of Germans belonging to the Kaiserin Augusta Guards Regiment, and splendidly led by a very brave officer, who shot L.-Cpl. Layburn through the head. The ability and determination of L.-Cpl. W. R. Cannon, M.M. and Bar, helped greatly during the subsequent fighting, for, with his Lewis gun, he killed the German officer, and thereafter dominated the situation. The advance to Black Wood was under direct observation from Battalion Headquarters, with whom communication was maintained throughout, by means of signal lamps. Their answering flashes were detected by the enemy, who caused a temporary cessation by well-directed machine-gun fire, but in a few minutes signalling was resumed, and the C.O. was able to send a "well done" to the men on the final objective.

A very pessimistic Guardsman captured during the day expressed his conviction that Germany was on the verge of collapse, and volunteered information that proved of great use to our Intelligence Corps.

At 2 a.m. on 29th August the line again moved forward, this time meeting with no opposition. By dawn our patrols had reached the outskirts of Flaucourt, overlooking the River Somme, and the town of Peronne, soon to be the scene of another Australian victory. The Seventh Australian Brigade then pushed through us, and continued the advance. The Transport and Quartermaster's Staff once more rose to the occasion, and soon the cookers were in line with the troops, providing a much-relished meal.

August 30th must be specially mentioned, if only for the fact that for twenty-four hours the Battalion rested. Dug-outs and shelters were fairly abundant and a good night's sleep, after a liberal rum issue, greatly helped in sustaining that high morale which was so noticeable a feature of this time.

On 31st August a move was made to a position in support near Clery-sur-Somme, and as much shelter as possible was procured from a high railway embankment there. There was a good deal of congestion here and some casualties were caused by shells. Capt. H. J. King and Lieut. A. W. Smith were among the wounded.

The Second Australian Division had now commenced that brilliant operation which eventually resulted in the capture of Mont St. Quentin, a most important tactical feature commanding Peronne and the Somme crossings there. At the time of Mont St. Quentin's capture a story obtained wide press publicity estimating the casualties sustained in the repeated attack as "ridiculously small." This statement was not at all in accordance with fact, for there was extremely stern fighting, first by the Fifth and then by the Sixth Brigades, before the latter finally captured and held the place. The casualty list was a long one.

Owing to being so constantly in action, the Twenty-Second Battalion was again the weakest, numerically, in the Sixth Brigade, and was used as Brigade Reserve. The Twenty-First, Twenty-Third, and Twenty-Fourth Battalions all co-operated together magnificently in the final attack and captured Mont St. Quentin, the carrying parties being supplied by the Twenty-Second. The night of the final attack our companies worked all night through barrages of gas and high explosive, delivering tools, ammunition, rations, and water to the front-line garrisons. Before dawn they took up a position in close support, as the enemy was expected to deliver strong counter-attacks.

On the evening of 1st September "A" and "B" Companies were in Gottlieb Trench, "C" Company was on the left of Haut Allines, junctioning there with an English Battalion on the Canal-du-Nord; while "D" Company, on the extreme right flank, occupied Gott Mit Uns Trench.

The Seventh Australian Brigade had now passed through and carried further objectives and this Battalion became attached to them for the purpose of covering the flanks which were exposed.

The Peronne operations by the Fifth Australian Division were now in full swing and the situation was often extremely obscure. "D" Company, though nominally in support at Gott Mit Uns Trench, at times found that they were close to active enemy posts, and several patrol encounters ensued, resulting in a number of prisoners being captured. Lieut. H. Thewlis was wounded during these operations. After the final capture of Peronne the situation cleared and the Company again passed into support. When the English Battalion on the left moved forward, "C" Company, who for two days had been doing front-line work, also became support troops.

On 4th September the Battalion was relieved and left the trenches to cross the Somme and bivouac at Boscourt. The route-marches of the

Kit and Kat, Westhoek.

next two days brought it to Cappy, the battle-ground of just eight days before, but now a comfortable and peaceful rest area.

Until 27th September a thoroughly good rest was enjoyed at Cappy and the three weeks of pleasant weather quickly passed. The distractions of this period included Divisional and Brigade Sports, Church Parades, and many ceremonial inspections.

A sweep consultation known as Tattersalls-sur-Somme was established under Divisional patronage, with War Bonds as prizes. Cpl. J. Ryan, of this Battalion, was fortunate enough to win one drawing, and received a bond for £100.

At football, Headquarters' team defeated the companies with great regularity.

One of the busiest men at this time was Sgt. Sturrock, who, with his confrere, Sgt. Gregory, went to no end of trouble to provide additional accommodation in our camp for the quota expected from the Twenty-First Battalion. The Higher Command had decided, owing to the shortage of man-power, to disband one Battalion in most of the Australian Brigades, and this melancholy lot was meditated for our gallant sister Battalion. The work of our pioneers was, however, in vain, as the expected quota never arrived. We dare not rob our comrades of the Twenty-First of the wealth of explanatory anecdote with which this period abounds. It is enough to say that the energetic measures they took at Cappy ensured their Battalion retaining its identity for some time longer, and in the last fight of the Brigade they added still further laurels to their great fighting record.

At the Brigade Sports on 14th September Driver Caffrey was our most successful representative in the pedestrian events, and Drivers Laidler and Flower persuaded our donks to great speed, finishing first and third in the mule race.

The Divisional Sports on the 16th September were a great success and boasted bookmakers, a totalisator, and a wet canteen.

At Cappy there was a widely-held opinion that the Battalion would not speedily return to the line, but confidence in this comforting theory was somewhat shaken when every night large bodies of troops moved linewards through the village.

Soon came rumours of future "stunts," and preparations were made for another move linewards. On 27th September, in the dark, the Battalion left Cappy, and, in order to avoid observation from enemy planes, continued by nightly stages, via Roisel, Villeret, and Marquaix.

On the evening of 1st-2nd October the final stage was made to Billiard Copse, near Nauroy. This last stage was made at short notice in intense darkness and without guides, with a compass bearing as the sole aid to direction. All the obstacles of the captured Hindenburg Line had to be crossed and the track lay across a deep canal and over difficult and entirely strange country. En route the moving companies were bombed by a low-flying German aeroplane, but no casualties resulted. The destination was reached soon after midnight, and great credit is due to Lieut. Harold Smith, M.C., M.M., for his expert work with map and compass under these unique conditions. Later in the night blankets and rations arrived and by daylight the Battalion was well dug in and as comfortable as the position permitted.

Billiard Copse lay well within the Hindenberg Line, and the adjacent village of Nauroy had been strongly fortified by the enemy. The trench systems here covered some thousands of yards in breadth and extended from the canal on the west to the Beaurevoir line on the east.

The Battalion remained at Billiard Copse until the afternoon of 3rd October.

CHAPTER XX.

BEAUREVOIR-MONT BREHAIN.—OCTOBER, 1918.

The Battalion's Last Fight.

During the month which had intervened between the Mont St. Quentin victory and the eve of the Battalion's re-appearance in the front line, the enemy's position had grown steadily worse. The third week of September had seen successful attacks launched against him on the whole British front, and during the last day of that month and the first two of October, the Hindenburg Line had been stormed from Le Catelet to Bellenglise. The Hun was still offering a stout resistance, but knowledge of the hopelessness of their cause was insidiously undermining the morale of his troops, while that of our own men rose correspondingly.

The position of Billiard Copse, where the Battalion found itself on 3rd October, has been described in the preceding chapter. East of it were the Beaurevoir defences, which were still held by the enemy. Orders for an attack on them were hourly expected.

These orders arrived at 3 p.m. on 3rd October in the form of instructions to move forward at once in readiness to attack, at an hour to be notified later, the German positions on the high ground to the right of the village of Beaurevoir, between the villages of Estrees and Geneve.

Though it was a bright, sunny afternoon, sunken roads and banks provided sufficient cover for a careful advance to the "J.O.T.," an old trench system crossing the Estrees-Geneve road. The moving columns were almost in position before they attracted the attention of a hostile aeroplane, and enemy 5.9's immediately shelled the area, fortunately causing only light casualties. The neighbourhood was ghastly and littered with enemy dead, the result of an attack early that day by the Fifth A.I. Brigade.

At 4.30 p.m., while movement to the "J.O.T.," was still in progress, our artillery put down a barrage and there were many surmises as to who was attacking. It was not ascertained until evening that this barrage was arranged to cover our own attack, which, unknown to us, had been arranged for 4.30 p.m. The horseman entrusted with this important message did not reach the Battalion, probably through no fault of his own, until 6.25 p.m. He then rode dramatically into the "waves" on the "J.O.T.," called for the C.O., and, proudly conscious of duty performed, regardless of personal danger, handed him this message:

"You will attack at 4.30 p.m."

A new arrangement had, however, meanwhile been arrived at whereby 6.30 p.m. was substituted as Zero hour, and this information arrived just seven minutes before that hour.

The Battalion was organised at this time on a three-company basis. "A" Company, who were on the left of the Estrees-Geneve road, facing the latter village, had for their objective a sunken road which ran between the road and La Motte Farm; "C" Company's mission was to push through this objective and, with "D" Company, who were on the right of the road, to capture and consolidate the high ground overlooking Geneve. On the Battalion's left flank was the Twenty-Fourth Battalion; on its right the Twenty-Third. The Battalion frontage amounted to 1400 yards, and it may safely be claimed that the feat of organising the companies in the seven minutes available between the receipt of orders and Zero hour, so that at 6.30 p.m. they moved off punctually and in splendid order, was only possible with a unit wherein all were highly trained and most were thoroughly experienced.

After a not very intense "eighteen-pounder" barrage of six minutes' duration, the "waves" pushed on through the isolated outposts of the Eighteenth Battalion, which were just beyond the "J.O.T." From those near the road came a warning cry, "Mind the quarry." The reference was to an excavation on the right of the road held by a strong garrison, all of whom, including a captain, the attackers bayoneted. The attack was made with such verve and initiative that, despite a strenuous resistance by enemy machine-gunners on the left flank, all objectives were quickly secured, along with one hundred prisoners, thirty machine-guns, four 77-mm. guns, and one 5.9 howitzer. This very decisive victory cost the Battalion only twenty casualties.

Amongst the killed, however, were two very well-known officers, Capt. W. Mc. Braithwaite, M.C., and Lieut. E. E. Patterson, M.C., both of whom had seen much heavy fighting with the Battalion. They commanded "C" and "D" Companies respectively in this engagement. The former, with No. 4374, Cpl. R. P. Bonnet, a very brave Lewis gunner of "C" Company, was killed in the act of charging a troublesome machine-

Hyde Park Corner, Ploegsteert.

gun. As the captain fell, those nearby heard his last order, "Go on, 'C' Company!" "C" Company lost another capable N.C.O. in No. 5625, Cpl. E. Light, and "D" Company a well-known identity in No. 1937, Pte. "Scotty" McAlpine, both of whom had seen much fighting. The latter was due for English leave, and it was a grim jest of fate that his leave pass should arrive at Battalion Headquarters just as news of his death came through from his company.

No deaths caused more poignant sorrow in the Battalion than those of the officers and men who fell during the last engagements, on the eve of a victory they were not to know.

The Transport and Q.M's. Staff again did good work and delivered rations and stores practically in the front line during the night of 3rd-4th October.

At 10.30 p.m. instructions came that the attack was to be continued in the morning, in conjunction with the Twenty-Third Battalion on the right and the Seventh British Brigade on the left. Between the latter and our Battalion ran the Torrens Canal, which served as a natural boundary for each unit.

The position was complicated by a change of direction in the attack, and the company positions had to be changed. "A" Company crossed from the left to the right of the Estrees-Geneve road, which thereafter became the boundary between them and "C" Company; "D" Company at the same time swung round to form a defensive flank along the Torrens Canal.

The above changes were effected in good order under cover of darkness, and the line that night swung back towards the left flank, where, in the morning, the British Brigade had to secure certain objectives before our Battalion began its advance. This entailed for our men a wait of twenty-five minutes on the "J.O.T." after the barrage opened on the morning of the 4th October, and with this warning of the attack that was obviously to follow, the enemy shelled the area heavily. Fortunately most of the shelling fell in the rear of the waiting men.

The struggle on the 4th was much more severe than that of the previous afternoon. The objectives fought for lay about Geneve, just beyond the road leading from that village to Montbrehain and to the right of Ponchaux, and though the first was gained without much difficulty, the second was captured only after much opposition from machine-gun fire. It was not without still more costly fighting that the final objective was carried. The task was made more difficult by heavy enemy fire from a factory south of Geneve, and the fact that the British Battalion which had penetrated into Ponchaux was unable to hold the village. Our left flank was exposed in consequence until the necessary arrangements for its defence were made by our companies. By 10 a.m. the Battalion had completely consolidated all its objectives.

The Battalion lost twenty-two killed and sixty-five wounded in this, its final, fight. The former included 2nd-Lieut. P. J. Dawsett, who had rejoined from an O.T.C. with his commission only a few days before.

A large number of prisoners was taken, and the booty included twenty machine-guns. This eminently successful and hotly contested action was a worthy finale to the Battalion's fighting record.

The 5th October was the last day spent by the Battalion in the firing line, for on the night of the 5th-6th October the One Hundred and Seventeenth American Regiment provided a relief.

The completion of this relief was delayed until the small hours of 6th October by a number of complications, and the Battalion can claim to have been one of the last—if not the last—Australian Infantry Battalion to be in the front line in France.

After a route-march to Roisel, the Battalion entrained there for St. Roch (Amiens), whence it marched twelve kilometres to billets at St. Vaast.

Major L. W. Matthews, D.S.O., and Sgt. W. Speechley, D.C.M., M.M., remained behind with the Americans for a few strenuous days.

The Battalion scored heavily in the matter of Honours awarded its officers and men for work done during the last fighting

For gallantry at Herleville, Lieuts. C. J. Fulton and E. Thewlis had received Military Crosses, and 1807, Sgt. W. Nash, the Distinguished Conduct Medal. Later, Military Crosses were awarded to Lieuts. P. G. Chalmers, G. T. Burrage, F. Howell, W. M. Proudfoot, K. Sutherland, and H. Smith, M.M., and a Bar to the Cross of Lieut. J. P. Green, M.C.

Among the winners of D.C.M's. were No. 2493, Sgt. R E. Batton; 2301a, Pte. M. W. Cowan, M.M.; 834, Cpl. H. Hayes, and 690, Sgt. W. Speechley, M.M., and a lengthy list of Military Medallists appeared shortly after the Battalion's last action.

CHAPTER XXI.

OCTOBER, 1918-MAY, 1919.

Last Days Abroad.

The little Somme hamlet of St. Vaast, where the Battalion was to spend an enjoyable and peaceful six weeks, was reached in the early hours of 8th October. The inhabitants were hospitable and billets good.

News of Allied victories reached us daily, and early in November it was evident that the enemy could not much longer postpone the admission of his defeat.

On 6th November warning orders were issued for the Battalion to prepare once more to take its place in the front of the battle, but the declaration of the Armistice on 11th November changed all such plans. Parades were in progress when the glad news came through, but all work ceased at once. The Band, liberally bedecked with floral tributes, paraded the streets and the Australian flag was hoisted on the church spire amid great manifestations of joy from the assembled villagers. The troops themselves accepted the news with singular calm, and apart from the inevitable nocturnal jollification, there were no demonstrations. It took days for men to realise that bloodshed and the hardships of service were to be no more, and that thoughts could at last be confidently turned towards "Home."

Battalion life soon resumed its even tenor. A platoon from "C" Company were runners-up in the Divisional Platoon Championship on 20th November, the Battalion thus gaining first and second places in the only two competitions of the kind ever held in the Second Australian Division. At a Divisional Horse Show the transport section carried off many prizes.

About the middle of November there were persistent rumours of an early move. These were followed by an official announcement (afterwards cancelled) that four Australian Divisions would move up to the Rhine territory, and the Battalion left St. Vaast on 22nd November, with high hopes of seeing the Hun on his native soil. The train journey from

Vigacourt to Bertry was on a par with many previous experiences of troop trains, and extended over twenty-four hours. From Bertry a march of many kilometres was made in the early hours of the 24th November to Bohain, a large town not far from the battlefield where the Battalion had fought its last action. The French inhabitants had many interesting but pitiful stories to tell of Hun callousness and oppression during the four years of their occupation, and the sight of the emaciated Allied prisoners who were returning daily from Germany was convincing enough evidence of their maltreatment in that country.

In the town itself, all metal and much clothing had been requisitioned and taken to Germany, forced labour had been recruited, and was obligatory on men and women alike to salute Hun officers under penalty of a substantial fine.

On 26th November the Battalion left Bohain and commenced a three-days' route-march to Boulogne-sur-Helpe, in the Avesnes area, via St. Souplet and Favril, at each of which semi-ruined villages a night was spent. It was between Boulogne and Avesnes that portion of the Battalion was reviewed on 1st December by His Majesty the King.

In the fortnight that followed there was nothing more exciting than a few closely contested inter-company football matches.

The duration of our stay had originally been estimated at a week, but it was not until 17th December that we commenced our march across the frontier into Belgium. Gourdinne, where the Battalion was to be billeted for two months, was reached on 19th December, and a hearty welcome was extended by the warm-hearted inhabitants, who had been eagerly awaiting our arrival. Shortly afterwards they formally presented an Address of Welcome to the Battalion on a ceremonial parade.

Preparations for our Xmas dinners were soon under weigh, and in these the local people evinced a lively interest. The dinners themselves, held in fine barns lit with electricity, will long live in the memories of those who were present.

A novelty was introduced for Headquarters' Dinner, when the Mademoiselles of Gourdinne kindly acted as waitresses, to the mutual satisfaction of the Company, their relatives, and themselves.

The dinners are aptly described in this extract from the War Diary of the period: "At their conclusion the men could not complain even of the bad weather; they were too full for words."

A sight of these gatherings would have gratified our friends of the Sixth Brigade Comforts Fund, who contributed so generously towards their cost.

LAST DAYS ABROAD.—OCTOBER, 1918-MAY, 1919

The Education Scheme had now become an established fact, and an officer was attached to the Battalion to superintend its workings. A number of officers and men left the unit on "non-military employment," and within the Battalion there were classes in half-a-dozen subjects. In addition, tours of inspection of the Charleroi industrial area were conducted at regular intervals, and a number of men were entered at workshops and schools of engineering.

Liberal leave was given to Charleroi, Brussels, Paris, and the United Kingdom, and yet the universal longing was for none of these so much as for Australia. "When are they going to send us home?" was the question uppermost in every mind.

A start was made on drafts for home when on Christmas Eve a small party of its married original members said farewell to their old Battalion. Larger drafts of veterans were despatched on 15th and 24th January. On each occasion they were accorded a fitting send-off; the Band played "Auld Lang Syne," and the Colonel shook hands with each man and wished him "bon voyage." Many of the old "originals" showed great emotion at the moment of parting and keenly felt the severance of their ties with the Regiment. In this they were not alone, and it may not be out of place to remark that as each draft marched out copious tears were shed by the mademoiselles of the village. These were renewed when on 13th February, 1919, the Battalion moved from Gourdinne to Marcinelle, a suburb of Charleroi. The regret we experienced at leaving was somewhat assuaged by the hospitality of our hosts in the new area.

Marcinelle is a prosperous locality, and the men were comfortably billeted. Charleroi proper is only a few hundred yards distant, and the troops were thus able to enjoy the distractions of a city as well as the comfort of home life with families who made them thoroughly welcome. This proximity to a large city—for the first time since Egyptian days—was greatly appreciated. Demobilisation was not rapid, but the continuance of liberal leave and numerous excursions to towns and places of interest made the time pass quickly.

Opportunities now offered of visiting Germany, and the Regimental Colours were sent up to Cologne to be dipped in the waters of the Rhine before being sent out to Australia. These Colours had been carried on all route-marches done after the Armistice. The first flag was dipped by the C.O. at 4 p.m. on 19th February, and two others at 6.30 p.m. on 18th March, 1919, by Lieut. H. Smith, M.C., M.M., and Lieut. E. Thewlis, M.C. In each case the Hohenzollern Bridge, Cologne, was the "scene of action." The Colours were immersed from the steps of a landing stage, and both times numbers of German civilians congregated and gazed with interest at the ceremony. The flags were brought back to Australia. One is in possession of the Twenty-Second Battalion C.M.F., Richmond, Victoria, and two others have been presented to the Australian War Museum.

On 6th April the Battalion despatched a draft of ninety men, made up for the most part by those who had left Australia in the first three months of 1916. On the eve of their departure the whole Battalion were present at a farewell dinner. Of the gradual demobilisation and return home of the remainder of our members it is not proposed to give detailed particulars, suffice it to say that in May a small cadre remained to convey the Battalion records to England. With the departure of these men the history of the Twenty-Second closes, a tranquil ending to a story of battle and striving.

In all about 8000 men passed through the old Battalion, and of these 850 laid down their lives in the cause of Right and Freedom. Its survivors, scattered all over the Commonwealth, will ever be proud of what their Regiment achieved. In the annals of the A.I.F. there will be no more more splendid pages than those which enshrine the traditions of the Twenty-Second, and which tell of sacrifices so willingly made and of hardships and dangers so bravely suffered.

Many long years hence, though the campaign may become but a memory, there will still survive in those who belonged to the Twenty-Second an abounding and justifiable pride in having served in what will always be to them the very "Best of Battalions."

THE END.

APPENDIX I.

TRANSPORT AT SALONIKA.

Contemporaneously with the Battalion's service on Gallipoli, its pack-drivers were engaged in another campaign, which on that account merits passing mention in these pages.

With the remainder of the 6th Brigade's first line transport, under Lieutenant W. M. Trew, 24th Battalion (afterwards Major Trew, D.S.O.), and ninety mules, they embarked at Alexandria on 31st August, 1915, on H.M.T. "Haverford" and sailed for Mudros with the "Southland," in the rescue of whose survivors the "Haverford" participated.

Instead of proceeding to Gallipoli with the Brigade, the pack-drivers, some fifty in number, were detained at Mudros for a month, and eventually attached to the Twelfth Irish Division, which had suffered heavily on the Peninsula, and was about to be despatched to the assistance of the Serbians.

With this Division they embarked for Salonika on the "Llandovery Castle," and on arrival were installed in Lambeth Camp, situated by the old Roman road running from Salonika to Constantiople. For the next three weeks employment was found for them as instructors in general pack work, and they themselves learned much from an observation of the methods employed by the Greeks, whose army had just been mobilised. At the end of that time they were distributed amongst the Dublins, Munsters, Leinsters, and 30th Brigade H.Qs. Shortly afterwards the Irish Division moved forward to Dorain, near the border of Greece and Serbia. The move was memorable on account of a "pay" in drachmas, prior to entrainment. These coins were accepted only at 50 per cent. discount once the border was crossed.

On the completion of the move, the attached Australians handed over their mules to the respective units and once more merged, thenceforth acting as a Divisional H.Q. Guard. The mules, to which they had devoted such attention, did not prove a success in the hilly country where they were now employed, and were soon exchanged for hardy mountain ponies.

Moving with the Divisional H.Q. our men made their first acquaintance with the active zone of operations at Hasanti. Their duties were varied, ranging from the care and collection of mountain ponies to the guarding of Bulgarian prisoners. The advent of winter found them at Fourk, where deserted habitations provided them with shelter from the elements and fuel for fires. When the Serbian retreat began the Australian party were at Dedile. Prior to the receipt of orders to withdraw their main energies were directed to the assistance of the numerous sufferers from frost-bite, who were painfully making their way back. The normal congestion involved in a retreat was aggravated by the narrowness of the roads and tracks. Progress to the objective—the Greek border near Lake Dorain—was slow, and often dangerous owing to steepness of declivities which bordered the route. On one occasion only one mile and a half were traversed in eleven hours, but the party with their ponies finally extricated themselves, and crossed the frontier. Lambeth Camp, their original resting place, was reached on 11th December.

The military situation was such that their services were no longer necessary, and they embarked for Alexandria on the mine sweeper "Folkestone." With two German spies in their custody they transhipped to the "Aragon," and in it were carried to their destination. In Egypt they rejoined their respective battalions. Included in the party of 22nd Battalion men who served in this campaign was Lieutenant F. Greenway, M.M. and Bar, whose decorations and commission were afterwards gained in France.

Pillbox occupied by Battalion Headquarters near Hannebeke.

APPENDIX II.

TOTAL CASUALTIES SUSTAINED BY 22nd BATTALION ON ACTIVE SERVICE.

	Killed.	Wounded.	Gassed.	P.O. War.	Sick.	Total.
Gallipoli	60	285	—	—	271	615
France	784	1888	288	44	1786	4790
	844	2173	288	44	2057	5406

Total killed: 46 officers, 798 other ranks.

APPENDIX III.

DECORATIONS

VICTORIA CROSS (V.C.).

2nd-Lieut. W. Ruthven.

MOST DISTINGUISHED ORDER OF ST. MICHAEL AND ST. GEORGE (CROSS). (C.M.G.).

Lieut.-Colonel A. R. L. Wiltshire, D.S.O., M.C.

DISTINGUISHED SERVICE ORDER (D.S.O.).

Major W. B. Craig.
Major L. W. Matthews.
Lieut.-Colonel A. R. L. Wiltshire, C.M.G., M.C.
Lieut.-Col. R. Smith (afterwards as G.O.C. 5th A.I. Brigade awarded C.M.G. and Bar to D.S.O.).

MILITARY CROSS (M.C.).

Capt. V. C. Alderson.
Lieut. P. J. Abercrombie.
Lieut. K. S. Anderson.
Lieut. E. T. Bazeley.
Lieut. W. McC. Braithwaite.
Lieut. G. T. Burrage.
Capt. W. H. Bunning.
Lieut. P. G. Chalmers.
Chaplain Rev. F. H. Durnford.
Capt. E. A. Davis.
Major J. S. Dooley.
Lieut. C. J. Fulton.
2nd-Lieut. F. Gawler.
Lieut. E. Gorman.
Lieut. J. P. Greene (awarded Bar to M.C., 10/12/18).
Lieut. A. Hughes.
Lieut. C. W. Hutton.
Lieut. L. W. Harricks.
Lieut. F. Howell.
2nd-Lieut. F. G. Kellaway.
2nd-Lieut. J. Kohn.
Capt. T. Millar.
Lieut. N. J. Madden.
Lieut. L. A. McCartin.
Capt. L. T. O. Pedler.
Lieut. E. E. Paterson.
Lieut. W. M. Proudfoot.
Capt. H. C. Rodda.
Capt. I. P. Stewart (awarded Bar to M.C., 31/10/17).
Lieut. A. Skene-Smith.
Lieut. K. Sutherland.
Lieut. H. Smith, M.M.
Lieut. E. Thewlis.
Lieut.-Col. A. R. L. Wiltshire, C.M.G., D.S.O.
Lieut. H. M. M. Wall.
2nd-Lieut. C. F. Yeadon.

APPENDIX

BAR TO MILITARY CROSS.

Lieut. J. P. Greene, M.C   Capt I. P. Stewart, M.C.

DISTINGUISHED CONDUCT MEDAL (D.C.M.).

2262 Pte. Bunting, W.M.
123 Sgt. Bregenzer, E.R.
2493 Sgt. Batton, R.E. (M.M. and Bar).
553 C.S.M. Blackmore, J.
342 C.S.M. Carter, T. S.
4669 R.S.M. Caldwell, S. (M.M.)
2301a Pte. Cowan, M. W. (M.M.)
2272 Sgt. Day, R. W. (M.M.)
603 Sgt. Good, L. G. A.
44449 Lance-Sgt. Gregory, P. T. (M.M.)
989 Pte. Horan, F.
4131 Sgt. Harris, W. C.
834 Cpl. Hayes, H. A.
2335 Pte. Hunt, O. P.
Lance-Cpl. Kruger, J.
4162 Sgt. Millar, A.
2347 Lance-Cpl. McFarlane, J. C.
2043 Pte. McKenna, A.
1807a Sgt. Nash, W.
47 Lance-Sgt. Nugent, E. R.
223 Pte. O'Neill, G. J.
3914 Sgt. Robinson, C. F.
1149 Sgt. Stone, R. G.
2398 Sgt. Strachan, T. G.
690 Sgt. Speechley, W. G. (M.M.)
1635 Pte. Weston, N. D.
1634 C.S.M. Werrett, R. C.
936 Pte. Warren, W.

BAR TO DISTINGUISHED CONDUCT MEDAL.

989 Cpl. Horan, F.

MERITORIOUS SERVICE MEDAL.

803 Sgt. Cox, C. F.
77 C.Q.M.S. Cugley, J. F.
242 Pte. Day, G. C.
832 R.Q.M.S. Hawkins, R. B.
1004 Sgt. King, J.
71 C.Q.M.S. Younger, S.W.

MILITARY MEDAL.

548 Pte. Adams, J. A.
323 Lance-Cpl. Aimers, W.
4653 Pte. Adams, E. H.
1114 Sgt. Armsden, A.
5539 Pte. Adams, G. A.
2493 Lance-Cpl. Batton, R. E.
4984 Pte. Bodsworth, L.
2260 Lance-Cpl. Baker, R. S.
1120 Pte. Beggs, L.
2460 Pte. Bain, D.
4361 Pte. Barnes, H. L.
117 Cpl. Binns, L. T.
4983 Lance-Sgt. Blatchford, C.
761 Lance-Cpl. Beckwith, S.
334 Sgt. Bridges, B. V.
4357 Pte. Baker, H. A.
4980 Pte. Binion, A. L.
5551 Pte. Benson, H. W.
1892 Lance-Cpl. Claridge, T. J.
1529 Pte. Cook, H. G.

APPENDIX

4670 Pte. Carroll, A.
3803 Pte. Cadman, A. L.
6055 Pte. Crawford, L.
4669 R.S.M. Cadwell, S.
1025 Cpl. Cannon, W. R.
2301 Pte. Cowan, M. W.
1217a Lance-Cpl. Cannard, F. J.
3809 Pte. Callaghan, A. B.
6052 Pte. Coleman, H. M.
5348 Pte. Douglas, J. T.
2272 Sgt. Day, R. W. (D.C.M.)
4699 Pte. Ellison, J.
1145 Pte. Fletcher, F. H.
6080 Pte. Friend, J. C.
1053 Cpl. Frowd, H. G.
1544 Sgt. Fraser, W. D.
4437 Lance-Cpl. Fry, C. R.
377 Sgt. Gallagher, G.
822 Pte. Greenway, F.
1679 Lance-Cpl. Greig, R. C. G.
4447 Pte. Green, G.
4710 Pte. Gilchrist, P. J.
160 Pte. Gorman, T.
5017 Sgt. Gould, A. W.
1719a Sgt. Gilchrist, S. C.
610 Sgt. Hayes, J. V.
1079 Pte. Hill, W. P.
401 Pte. Hull, O. J.
1060 Sgt. Hughes, G. C.
4723 Pte. Hughes, W. E.
2884a Pte. Holloway, G. H. B
1146 Pte. Hewitson, J. J.
4133 Lance-Cpl. Harris, F. C.
1159 Temp.-Cpl. Hecker, H. L.
5362 Pte. Hanks, F. N.
6093 Pte. Hanlon, M. J.
1058 Sgt. Horman, W. J.
1077 Pte. Ilett, R.
1737 Pte. Jones, F.
1161 Cpl. Johns, J. H.
1915 Cpl. Jinks, M. D.
5890 Pte. Jane, R. F.

505 Lance-Cpl. Kenyon, G. M.
6109 Pte. Konza, E.
6837 Lance-Sgt. Kennett, J. S.
6376 Lance-Cpl. Kaye, N. E.
181 Lance-Cpl. Kirby, F. V.
1920 Pte. Kelly, H.
29 Pte. Lambourne, J. F.
4531a Pte. Lucas, H. R.
967 Pte. Lindsay, F.
5117 Pte. Layburn, W. J. A.
4478 Cpl. Lambert, J.
1980 Sgt. Massey, H. V.
78 Sgt. Monaghan, G. L.
859 Pte. Morey, L. C.
1109 Pte. Martin, C.
641 Lance-Cpl. Moore, V. N.
636 Pte. Martin, P. V.
5056 Pte. Merson, H. S.
2176 Cpl. Moore, C. R.
4490 Pte. Matthews, W. F.
1644 Lance-Cpl. Marum, A. W.
5811 Temp.-Cpl. Marsh, J.
646 Lance-Sgt. Moodie, W. S. R.
6862 Pte. McKenzie, P.
6401 Lance-Cpl. McColl, J. P.
1707a Pte. McKenzie, G. A.
1936 Pte. McAlpine, A. J.
5395 Cpl. McDonald, R.
2293 Temp.-Cpl. McMillan, K.
2300 Sgt. Nichols, H. J.
663 Sgt. O'Beirne, J.
520 Cpl. O'Neill, L. T.
1942 Lance-Cpl. Oldfield, O. W.
6273 Cpl. O'Farrell, J. P.
6865 Pte. O'Bree, J. T.
443 Pte. O'Connor, W.
224 Pte. Parker, T. E.
5075 Pte. Penman, J. T.
2488 Pte. Robbins, G.
2019 Pte. Rutter, A.
5660 Pte. Ross, J.
4199 Cpl. Riley, T. W. F.

APPENDIX

1727 Lance-Cpl. Rutter, W. G.
 680 Sgt. Rowden, T. F.
 681 Lance-Cpl. Russell, L.
 235 Dvr. Rhodes, A.
5818 Pte. Rogan, C. F.
 690 Sgt. Speechley, W. G.
2396 Sgt. Swift, H. P.
4474 Pte. Smith, P. E.
4542 Pte. Splatt, V. E.
5686 Lance-Cpl. Strawhorn, L.
 457 Lance-Sgt. Schammer, W.
4538 Cpl. Shimkovich, E.
1031 Pte. Spokes, W. E.
2398 Sgt. Strachan, T. G. (D.C.M.)
4791 Pte. Stillman, J.
5911 Pte. Shields, J.
6149 Pte. Stevenson, H.
2394 Pte. Stephens, G. T.
 919 Pte. Strain, J. F.
1779 Cpl. Schaefer, P.
1063 Pte. Small, H. N.
 529 Pte. Sands, F. C.
 462 Pte. Smith, E. R.
 695 Pte. Smith, H.
1043 Pte. Smith, S.

1069 Pte. Tucker, C.
1187 Cpl. Tourrier, W. A.
2438 Lance-Cpl. Tripp, G. H. R.
1627 Sgt. Trewartha, C. L.
5919 Lance-Cpl. Tytler, S. J.
 699 Lance-Sgt. Thurlow, P.
4558 Pte. Taylor, A. V.
 770a Pte. Tuddin, W.
6165 Pte. Varrie, W.
 547 Pte. Wootton, S.
2051 Pte. Wright, J.
5691 Pte. Wilton, C. T.
 753 Sgt. Watkins, E. F.
3957 Pte. Walkerden, A.
 285 Pte. Williams, P.
3969 Sgt. Waxman, C. R.
6166 Lance-Sgt. Woolston, N. F.
6171 Pte. Wilson, C. C.
5715 Pte. Watson, T.
5431 Lance-Sgt. West, C. G.
4799 Cpl. West, F. S.
 914 Pte. Wood, A. P.
2012a Pte. White, A. T.
 530 Lance-Cpl. Young, W. J.
2416 Cpl. Thomas, J. A.

BAR TO MILITARY MEDAL.

2493 Sgt. Batton, R. E., D.C.M., M.M.
 117 Cpl. Binns, L. T.
1025 Cpl. Cannon, W. R.
 160 Cpl. Gorman, T.
1719a Sgt. Gilchrist, S. C.

 646 Lance-Sgt. Moodie, W. S. R.
5056 Lance-Cpl. Merson, H. S.
1707a Pte. McKenzie, G. A.
6273 Cpl. O'Farrell, J. P.
4799 Cpl. West, F. S.
5691 Pte. Wilton, C. F.

MENTIONED IN DESPATCHES.

Lieut. P. J. Abercrombie, M.C.
Lieut. K. S. Anderson, M.C. (twice).
Major H. A. Crowther.
Major N. M. Mackay.

Capt. D. T. Miles.
Capt. T. Millar, M.C.
Major L. W. Matthews, D.S.O.
Lieut. R. P. Penna.
Capt. H. C. Rodda, M.C.

Lieut.-Col. R. Smith, D.S.O.
Capt. J. H Slater
Capt. I. P. Stewart, M.C.
2nd-Lieut. S. J. Wicks.
Lieut.-Colonel A. R. L. Wiltshire, C.M.G., D.S.O., M.C. (three times).
760 Pte. Blow, C.
342 C.S.M. Carter, T. S.
4669 R.S.M. Cadwell, S., D.C.M., M.M.
588 Lance-Cpl. Dyett, S.C.
2272 Sgt. Day, R. W.
398 Lance-Cpl. Heffernan, J.
636 Pte. Martin, P. V., M.M.
216 Pte. Murray, T. J.
201 Lance-Sgt. Mackenzie, T.
230 R.S.M. Porter, R. E.
461 Lance-Cpl. Smart, E. C.
2368 Pte. Simkins, J. L.
699 Lance-Sgt. Thurlow, P., M.M.
1634 C.S.M. Werrett, R. C., D.C.M.
6171 Pte. Wilson, C. C.

FOREIGN DECORATIONS.
OFFICIER DE L'ORDRE DE LEOPOLD (BELGIUM).

Lieut.-Colonel D. M. Davis.

SERBIAN SILVER MEDAL.

1529 Pte. Cook, H. G. (M.M.)
335 Lance-Cpl. Bridges, E. C.
1037 Pte. Allum, R.

ST. GEORGE'S CROSS OF RUSSIA.

1635 Pte. Weston, N. D. (D.C.M.)

FRENCH CROIX DE GUERRE.

2151 Sgt. Harwood, J.

BELGIAN CROIX DE GUERRE.

4669 R.S.M. Caldwell, S. (D.C.M., M.M.)
6044 Pte. Brodie, L. A.
1681 C.S.M. Castledine, F. R.

APPENDIX

SUMMARY.

V.C.	1
C.M.G.	1
D.S.O.	4
M.C.	36
D.C.M.	22
M.M.	154
M.S.M.	6
Foreign	9

BARS.

M.C.	2
D.C.M.	1
M.M.	11
	253

Mentioned in Despatches .. 25

ROLL OF HONOUR

Dulce et decorum est pro patria mori

No.	Rank.	Name.	Date of Death.	Cause of Death.
845	Pte.	LAUDER, J.	3/6/15	Illness
740	,,	KAY, T.	14/6/15	Accident
466	,,	SOMMERVILLE, H. G.	18/7/15	Illness
297	,,	BUNTING, E. A.	28/7/15	,,
1023	,,	DEAN, J. W. W.	3/8/15	,,
115	,,	BARTON, F.	23/8/15	,,
1106	,,	SAMWAYS, W. S.	15/9/15	Killed in Action
787	,,	BROUGHTON, T. G.	24/9/15	Illness
1690	,,	HOTHAM, A. J.	17/9/15	Died of Wounds
1685	,,	HEARD, A. J.	17/9/15	Killed in Action
1217	,,	WATKINS, W. H.	18/9/15	,, ,,
151	,,	ELLIOTT, A. J.	18/9/15	,, ,,
608	,,	GAUNT, P.	12/9/15	Died of Wounds
1236	Dvr.	KERR, J. C. M.	14/10/15	Illness
1555	Pte.	HINDS, W. H.	14/10/15	,,
	Major	DERRICK, C. R.	20/9/15	Died of Wounds
65	Pte.	NEWBOUND, G. A.	1/10/15	,, ,,
1558	,,	JOHNSON, A.	1/10/15	Killed in Action
889	,,	RANDALL, F. H.	1/10/15	,, ,,
1008	,,	HANLEY, M.	2/10/15	Died of Wounds
677	,,	RHODES, J. H. W.	4/10/15	,, ,,
605	,,	GRANT, H.	4/10/15	,, ,,
812	,,	DURANCE, E. W.	4/10/15	,, ,,
644	,,	MARSH, R. W. S.	18/9/15	,, ,,
562	,,	BELLESINI, H.	18/9/15	,, ,,
732	,,	CROWTHER, A.	2/11/15	,, ,,
124	,,	BROOKS, G.	13/10/15	Killed in Action
459	,,	SCOTT, J. K.	14/10/15	Illness
582	,,	CHENERY, A. G.	24/10/15	Died of Wounds
1512	,,	BRAIN, E. G.	24/10/15	Illness
500	,,	DAVIS, E. W.	17/10/15	Killed in Action
288	,,	WITHERS, W. E.	15/9/15	Illness
691	,,	SUMMERSFORD, R.	22/10/15	Died of Wounds
501	,,	FRASER, D. D.	10/10/15	"Gassed"
1960	,,	STELLING, G.	29/10/15	Killed in Action
411	Cpl.	KEAST, T. E. C.	27/10/15	,, ,,
470	L.-Cpl.	SYMMONS, H.	27/10/15	,, ,,
92	Pte.	GOOD, W. B. S.	29/10/15	"Gassed"
308	L.-Cpl.	LOOKER, F. K.	15/11/15	Illness
1223	,,	FRICKER, P. T.	16/11/15	,,
480	Pte.	TODD, J. W.	5/11/15	Died of Wounds
198	,,	McDONALD, J. H.	27/10/15	,, ,,
1180	,,	COX, J. W. E.	3/11/15	Killed in Action
231	,,	PRICE, W.	21/11/15	Died of Wounds
516	,,	McCLURE, A. D.	20/11/15	,, ,,

ROLL OF HONOUR

No.	Rank.	Name.	Date of Death.	Cause of Death.
1944	Pte	PORTER, H. T.	24/11/15	Illness
2005	”	SMITH, P. L.	21/11/15	Killed in Action
1636	”	WHITE, J. L.	12/11/15	Illness
193	”	LONG, A. B.	16/11/15	Killed in Action
1801	”	WRIGHT, H. P.	21/11/15	Died of Wounds
1904	”	HAMILTON, F. G.	6/12/15	Illness
275	”	WALSH, J. T.	7/12/15	” ”
1623	”	THOMSON, W. D.	8/12/15	Died of Wounds
1196	”	WEBSTER, W. J.	27/11/15	Killed in Action
1906	”	HOBBS, A.	2/12/15	” ”
804	L.-Cpl.	CRANE, H.	13/8/16	Died of Wounds
797	Pte.	COBHAM, R.	13/9/15	Illness
1957	”	SMART, G. W.	3/12/15	Died of Wounds
273	L.-Cpl.	WALLACE, P. A.	15/4/16	” ”
1549	Pte.	JORDAN, R. J.	15/4/16	Accident
	Capt.	BUCKLEY, H. C.	27/4/16	Died of Wounds
825	Pte.	HALL, G.	27/4/16	Killed in Action
	Lieut.	KING, J. B.	5/5/16	Died of Wounds
2302	Pte.	PATTERSON, J. H.	3/6/16	” ”
823	”	GREENWOOD, J. H.	21/6/16	Killed in Action
506	”	HAMILTON, J. B.	24/6/16	” ”
2340	”	HOSKING, H.	24/6/16	” ”
2339	”	HOGAN, M. J.	24/6/16	Died of Wounds
503	”	EVANS, W. R.	24/6/16	” ”
2305	”	PRIDHAM, A. T.	23/6/16	Killed in Action
1784	”	SANDERSON, J. W.	27/4/16	Died of Wounds
2013	L.-Cpl.	WYLIE, D. J.	1/7/16	” ”
	Lieut.	OLDFIELD, L.	26/6/16	” ”
120	Pte.	BLACKLEY, W.	24/6/16	” ”
2306	”	WHITE, A.	23/6/16	Killed in Action
2237	”	AUSTIN, T.	27/6/16	” ”
831	”	HARLE, J. B.	27/6/16	” ”
2121	”	BELL, E.	30/6/16	Died of Wounds
498	L.-Cpl.	WYETH, G.	23/3/16	Killed in Action
502	Pte.	ELLIOTT, E.	2/7/16	Accident
4381	Cpl.	BRODIE, J. D.	15/7/16	Illness
4099	Pte.	VIDLER, E. G.	27/7/16	Died of Wounds
	2nd Lieut.	TAPNER, B. S.	29/7/16	Killed in Action
	”	SCANLON, H. D.	5/8/16	” ”
	Capt.	HART, A.	5/8/16	” ”
	2nd Lieut.	CURNOW, H. F.	5/8/16	” ”
	”	THOMAS, H. N.	”	” ”
383	Pte.	CONDON, R.	6/8/16	” ”
	Lieut.	GRANT, J.	17/8/16	Died of Wounds
	2nd Lieut.	KENNETT, C.	17/8/16	” ”
3995	Pte.	McKAY, E. B.	28/7/16	” ”
3820	”	WHITESIDE, W.	31/7/16	” ”
2132	”	DALE, A.	27/7/16	” ”
3762	”	CLARKE, H. I.	27/7/16	” ”
1116	L.-Cpl.	BLOOMER, F. N.	5/8/16	” ”
41	Pte.	KIRBY, W. F.	28/7/16	” ”
2216	”	COOK, F. E.	31/7/16	” ”
922	”	REGAN, F.	31/7/16	” ”
2445	”	THOMAS, J.	30/7/16	” ”
	2nd Lieut.	WELLS, A.	8/8/16	” ”
		YATES, A. W.		” ”

ROLL OF HONOUR

No.	Rank.	Name.	Date of Death.	Cause of Death.
1156	Pte.	KIRKWOOD, W. J. C.	5/8/16	Killed in Action
4591	,,	LOGAN, E. R. W.	5/8/16	,, ,,
3821	,,	DALEY, J.	5/8/16	,, ,,
1148	Sgt.	PEART, E. M.	30/7/16	Died of Wounds
27	Pte.	KENNEDY, W.	30/7/16	,, ,,
1126	L.-Cpl.	DAWES, W. J.	5/8/16	Killed in Action
1976	Pte.	HAYES, J. H.	5/8/16	,, ,,
3781	,,	BATH, A. F.	5/8/16	,, ,,
1178	,,	BOWDEN, W. G.	5/8/16	,, ,,
2264	,,	COSTELLO, H. J.	5/8/16	,, ,,
1741	L.-Cpl.	TOPPING, A. E.	10/8/16	Died of Wounds
248	Pte.	SMITH, W.	7/8/16	,, ,,
4235	,,	WALSH, M. A.	7/8/16	,, ,,
310	,,	SINCLAIR, E. A.	27/7/16-4/8/16	Killed in Action
3915	,,	RUTTER, A. E.	,,	,, ,,
1933	,,	MATHEWS, E. G.	,,	,, ,,
191	,,	LINDSAY, J.	,,	,, ,,
2173	L.-Cpl.	LAPTHORNE, W. F.	,,	,, ,,
3861	Pte.	KENDALL, J. B.	,,	,, ,,
1205	,,	HARDMAN, C. E.	,,	,, ,,
1903	,,	HART, H. E.	,,	,, ,,
2331	,,	GARDINER, J.	,,	,, ,,
3610	,,	CURTIS, S. J.	,,	,, ,,
137	,,	CRONIN, P. F.	,,	,, ,,
1122	,,	BULMAN, H.	,,	,, ,,
2488	,,	ROBBINS, G. E.	,,	,, ,,
2094	,,	WARD, E. C.	,,	,, ,,
1610	,,	SHARP, C. W.	,,	,, ,,
242	Sgt.	SELLGREN, C. J. L.	5/8/16	,, ,,
4409	Pte.	DAWSON, H. G.	,,	,, ,,
3946	,,	SELLENS, W. E.	5/8/16	Killed in Action
2112	L.-Cpl.	RUDDICK, W. N.	,,	,, ,,
1207	Cpl.	RASHLEIGH, H. G.	,,	,, ,,
215	,,	MURPHY, J. J.	,,	,, ,,
3879	Pte.	MORGAN, G.	,,	,, ,,
1149	Sgt.	STONE, R. G. (D.C.M.)	27/7/16	,, ,,
2309	Pte.	SHAW, R. W.	,,	,, ,,
319	,,	MASON, A. E.	,,	,, ,,
2358	,,	ROWAN, J. T.	27/7/16-4/8/16	,, ,,
1105	,,	ROBSON, W. O.	,,	,, ,,
673	,,	POPLE, H.	,,	,, ,,
2037	L.-Cpl.	MORGAN, H. J.	7/8/16	Died of Wounds
337	,,	BURKE, T. D.	6/8/16	,, ,,
4438	Pte.	ISAACS, W. W.	5/8/16	Killed in Action
4442	,,	GILLIN, W. M.	22/8/16	Died of Wounds
107	,,	ANDREWS, E. E.	5/8/16	Killed in Action
1878	,,	ANDERSON, F.	,,	,, ,,
2174	,,	LYAL, J. G.	,,	,, ,,
774	,,	MOORE, R. C. T.	,,	,, ,,
203	,,	McLEOD, C. J.	,,	,, ,,
437	,,	McKINNON, C. J.	,,	,, ,,
1539	,,	ELLIS, E.	,,	,, ,,
1082	,,	JOHNSON, T.	,,	,, ,,
739	,,	HATCHER, W. L.	7/8/16	Died of Wounds
365	,,	DRAFFIN, A. V.	,,	,, ,,
4124	,,	HOGAN, E. W.	6/8/16	,, ,,

ROLL OF HONOUR

No.	Rank.	Name.	Date of Death.	Cause of Death.
3324	Sgt.	WILLIAMS, A. R.	5/8/16	Killed in Action
3971	Pte.	WEIR, T.	"	" "
270	"	WALL, J.	"	" "
268	"	VIENNA, E.	"	" "
1972	"	TAIT, P. J.	5/8/16	Killed in Action
2411	"	SELLWOOD, L. J.	"	" "
1546	"	GEORGE, J.	27/7/16-4/8/16	" "
820	"	GANDER, J. H.	"	" "
118	"	BIRCH, C. J.	"	" "
104	"	ADKINS, A. R.	"	" "
2554	"	ANDREWS, C. H.	6/8/16	Died of Wounds
872	"	NELSON, W. J.	29/7/16	" "
188	"	LEVER, F. D.	28/7/16	" "
2384	"	SAXON, F. C.	22/7/16	" "
1096	L.-Cpl.	SEAMARK, G.	30/7/16	" "
2319	Pte.	STEWART, B.	9/8/16	" "
197	"	McDERMOTT, J.	1/8/16	" "
2620a	"	CHANTER, A. E.	25/7/16	Killed in Action
159	"	GLOVER, A. W.	11/8/16	Died of Wounds
1643	"	WALKER, C.	10/8/16	" "
332	Sgt.	BISHOP, R. E.	11/8/16	" "
3257	Pte.	SMYTHE, W.	25/7/16	Killed in Action
2563	"	BAILEY, C. H.	"	" "
3199	Sgt.	McLEAN, D.	"	" "
2665	Pte.	HONAN, E. J.	"	" "
3218	"	PRATT, C. E.	"	" "
	Major	MACKAY, M. N.	5/8/16	" "
884	Pte.	PENROSE, J. F.	27/7/16-4/8/16	" "
100	"	NEWTON, I.	"	" "
2344	"	MIDDLETON, E. H.	"	" "
2296	"	McTAVISH, D. W.	"	" "
1554	"	McCANN, H. J. B.	"	" "
2216	"	ARMISTEAD, E. J.	"	" "
2320	"	THOMPSON, W. J.	"	" "
615a	"	DOVE, W. J.	"	" "
175	Sgt.	WOOD, E. C.	"	" "
2478	Pte.	WILSON, L. A.	"	" "
2507	"	WARDLE, W. E.	27/7/16-4/8/16	Killed in Action
1762	"	HODSON, J. J.	4/8/16	" "
4441	"	GILLIN, T. H.	28/8/16	" "
377	Sgt.	GALLAGHER, G. D. A.	11/8/16	Died of Wounds
2158	Pte.	BARNETT, W.	16/8/16	" "
4150	"	KEANE, J. L.	24/8/16	" "
924	"	THORNEYCROFT, D.	"	Killed in Action
207	"	SMITH, J. B.	26/8/16	" "
462	"	SMITH, E. R.	"	" "
271	"	WALL, R.	8/8/16	" "
631	"	McKENZIE, L. F. J. A.	7/8/16	Died of Wounds
1726a	"	ROWE, E. C.	30/8/16	" "
	Capt.	SMITH, H. E.	25/8/16	" "
1793	Pte.	GUTTERSON, C.	26/8/16	Killed in Action
1112	"	ALLATT, A. H.	26/8/16	Died of Wounds
901	Cpl.	COUSTLY, E.	"	Killed in Action
4549	Temp. Sgt.	SUMNER, J.	"	" "
1069	Temp. Cpl.	TUCKER, C. S.	"	" "
349	Pte.	COLTMAN, P. E.	5/8/16	" "

ROLL OF HONOUR

No.	Rank.	Name.	Date of Death.	Cause of Death.
4406	Pte.	DARCEY, M.	5/8/16	Killed in Action
4101	"	DUFFY, A. P.	"	" "
3889	"	McKENZIE, J. J.	"	" "
3767	"	BURNIE, C.	24/8/16	" "
433	Sgt.	MUNTZ, E. G.	5/8/16	" "
1772	Pte.	LUMSDEN, C. A.	2/6/16	Illness
61	S. Sgt.	WILLIAMSON, H.	6/8/16	Died of Wounds
985	Pte.	EVANS, H.	7/8/16	" "
2266	"	CARTER, W.	6/8/16	" "
4580	"	ARMITAGE, A. C.	13/10/16	" "
514	L.-Cpl.	LE MAITRE, A. C.	5/8/16	Killed in Action
4373	Pte.	BOLLOM, E. W.	30/10/16	" "
2368	"	SIMKIN, J. L.	15/8/16	Illness
3771	"	BENSLEY, E. H.	12/11/16	Died of Wounds
4393	"	CLEARY, W.	11/11/16	" "
	2nd Lieut.	McCORMICK, N. W.	7/11/16	Died of Wounds
1579	Pte.	MOORE, T. J.	3/11/16	Killed in Action
2388	"	SCHWAB, C. H.	8/8/16	Died of Wounds
2356	L.-Cpl.	QUINN, A. A.	16/11/16	" "
830	"	HARDING, S. F.	19/11/16	" "
5968	Pte.	COLLETT, J. M.	27/11/16	" "
4520	"	PHAIR, H. W.	25/11/16	Illness
333	Sgt.	BLEECHMORE, D.	5/8/16	Died of Wounds
3960	Pte.	WEIR, J. J.	15/11/16	Killed in Action
4541	"	SNEDDON, L.	7/11/16	" "
4466	"	HUTCHISON, C. H.	8/11/16	" "
634	L.-Cpl.	McLEAN, W. R.	"	" "
2459	Pte.	BISHOP, A. E.	12/11/16	" "
4767	"	McLACHLAN, J. J.	13/11/16	" "
265	"	TURNER, F.	17/11/16	" "
4730	"	JULIAN, W. C.	"	" "
4137	"	HUMPHRIES, W.	"	" "
4765	"	McFARLANE, T. B.	15/11/16	" "
879	"	PARK, A.	13/11/16	" "
1882	"	BECK, J.	3/8/16	" "
	2nd Lieut	PRITCHARD, L. B.	15/8/16	" "
5018	Pte.	GRATTON, S. J.	14/12/16	" "
4495	"	MOLONEY, J. R.	15/12/16	Illness
348	"	COBBAN, B.	27/7/16	" "
2285	"	JONES, J. (Alias SCANNELL, J. E.)	5/8/16	Killed in Action
394	"	HAWKINS, A. B.	27/7/16	" "
2292	L.-Cpl.	McGILL, H. S.	"	" "
980	"	LUTEY, V. P.	4/8/16	" "
1628	Pte.	WALKER, G. H.	5/8/16	" "
2323	"	WHITE, H. J.	"	" "
2221	Cpl	ROBINSON, F.	4/1/17	Died of Wounds
5000	L.-Cpl.	CURTAIN, J. J.	3/1/17	" "
4246	Pte.	CHAMBERLAIN, L. V.	2/1/17	Killed in Action
4780	"	QUINN, A. O.	15/11/16	" "
4452	"	HAM, W. F.	23/11/16	Died of Wounds
6177	"	CANHAM, H. C.	28/1/17	Illness
1744	"	LOCARNINI, C. B.	20/2/17	" "
4465	L.-Sgt.	HURTER, E. C. T.	7/2/17	Killed in Action
5315	Pte.	BIBER, F. W.	10/2/17	" "
5371	"	JAGO, G. E.	"	" "

ROLL OF HONOUR

No.	Rank.	Name.	Date of Death.	Cause of Death.
4583	Pte.	KAVANAGH, T.	10/2/17	Killed in Action
5459	,,	MATSON, W. L.	,,	,, ,,
5300	,,	LE BON, E. G.	3/3/17	Died of Wounds
37	,,	KRUGER, J. H.	26/2/17	Injuries
3963	Temp. Cpl.	WITTNER, H.	21/2/17	Killed in Action
817	Cpl.	FIRTH, D. H.	5/8/16	,, ,,
153	Sgt.	FLEMING, P.	25/2/17	,, ,,
4421	L.-Cpl.	DWYER, G. B.	25/2/17	,, ,,
4971	Pte.	ALEXANDER, C. B.	25/2/17	,, ,,
4174	,,	McGANN, H. N.	11/3/17	Died of Wounds
3950	,,	TAYLOR, H. E.	5/8/16	Killed in Action
1714	C.S.M.	OLDHAM, F. H.	11/3/17	Illness
4132	Pte.	HEYME, G. T.	5/8/16	Killed in Action
	Lieut.	CORNE, W.	26/2/17	,, ,,
5356	Pte.	GOODALL, J. B.	9/3/17	,, ,,
4497	,,	MOORE, C. P.	10/3/17	,, ,,
2391	Cpl.	SIDDELL, J. W.	16/3/17	,, ,,
76	Pte.	CORNISH, P. J.	29/3/17	Illness
3864	,,	LANDER, R.	12/3/17	Killed in Action
1630	,,	WYNN, J.	15/3/17	,, ,,
994	,,	SUMMERSFORD, A.	17/4/17	,, ,,
320	,,	MAWDSLEY, T.	25/4/17	Died of Wounds
1081	Dvr.	HOLMAN, G. B.	6/8/16	Killed in Action
5111	Pte.	WINTER, B. J.	15/4/17	,, ,,
1991	L.-Cpl.	ANDERSON, A.	17/4/17	,, ,,
5008	Pte.	FOWLES, E. H.	16/4/17	,, ,,
5019	,,	GROVES, L.		,, ,,
4562	,,	VASS, W. C. J.	17/4/17	,, ,,
5351	,,	FRY, H.		,, ,,
	Lieut.	GREIG, W. C.	30/4/17	Died of Wounds
393	Sgt.	HAMILTON, N. W.	5/8/16	Killed in Action
379	Pte.	LUCK, E. S.	21/4/17	,, ,,
5793	,,	ELLIS, C.	5/5/17	Died of Wounds
5978	,,	LYNCH, P. J.	6/5/17	,, ,,
2182	L.-Cpl.	MARSHALL, W.	3/5/17	,, ,,
3819	Pte.	DWYER, J.	4/5/17	,, ,,
5845	,,	BOURCHIER, E. D.	3/5/17	,, ,,
4777	,,	POWELL, H. C.	4/5/17	,, ,,
2232	,,	TAYLOR, R. H.	4/5/17	,, ,,
	Capt.	SLATER, J. H.	3/5/17	Killed in Action
	Lieut.	SCAMMELL, S.	3/5/17	,, ,,
	2nd Lieut.	GRIFFIN, J.	3/5/17	,, ,,
	,,	FILMER, W. S.	,,	,, ,,
1945	Temp. Cpl.	REES, J. H.	8/5/17	Died of Wounds
4455	Pte.	HEALEY, L. C.	9/5/17	,, ,,
5022	,,	GUNN, W.	17/5/17	,, ,,
4787	,,	SEARLE, W. A.	6/5/17	,, ,,
6072	,,	DITTON, J. P.	3/5/17	Killed in Action
149	L.-Cpl.	DYER, H. S.	,,	,, ,,
5098a	Pte.	FREEMAN, D. L. de C.	,,	,, ,,
5584	,,	FRY, T.	,,	,, ,,
378	,,	GARBELLINI, G.	,,	,, ,,
4721	L.-Cpl.	HARRIS, E. A.	,,	,, ,,
1912	Sgt.	HUNTER, D.	,,	,, ,,
5600	Pte.	HALLAND, T. F.	,,	,, ,,
1732	L.-Cpl.	HARRISON, A. C.	,,	,, ,,

ROLL OF HONOUR

No.	Rank.	Name.	Date of Death.	Cause of Death.
3862	Pte.	KIERULF, H. O.	3/5/17	Killed in Action
5474	,,	KYLE, A. R.	,,	,, ,,
4743	,,	LYNCH, T.	,,	,, ,,
5377	,,	LAFRANCHI, P.	,,	,, ,,
5050	,,	LYTE, H. A.	,,	,, ,,
4159	,,	MABBITT, B. J.	,,	,, ,,
5869	Cpl.	MAINE, L. C.	,,	,, ,,
5895	Pte.	MARSHALL, P. J.	,,	,, ,,
2474	,,	MARTIN, C. N.	,,	,, ,,
4751	,,	MOONEY, J. W.	,,	,, ,,
5630	,,	MORFEE, W. G.	,,	,, ,,
5080	,,	PURCELL, J. R.	,,	,, ,,
683	,,	RANDS, A.	,,	,, ,,
2359	,,	REYNOLDS, D. T.	,,	,, ,,
4182	,,	OAKLEY, T. B.	,,	,, ,,
5407	,,	ROBINS, H. P.	,,	,, ,,
1612	,,	SHIELDS, H. V.	,,	,, ,,
2440	L.-Cpl.	TEICHELMAN, N.	,,	,, ,,
5420	Pte.	TREGLOWN, A. A.	,,	,, ,,
2425	L.-Cpl.	TRIGG, T. A.	,,	,, ,,
5423	Pte.	TURNER, E. P.	,,	,, ,,
3958	,,	WEALAND, N. D.	,,	,, ,,
5833	L.-Cpl.	WELCH, E. W.	,,	,, ,,
4802	Sgt.	WHITE, J. J.	,,	,, ,,
3996	Cpl.	WILSON, F. W.	,,	,, ,,
5110	Pte.	WINNELL, C.	,,	,, ,,
5960	,,	WYLIE, H.	,,	,, ,,
3854	,,	JOHNSTON, R.	,,	,, ,,
4488	,,	MARTIN, S. C.	,,	,, ,,
5107	,,	WILSON, D. G.	,,	,, ,,
111	L.-Cpl.	BAKER, A. E. L.	,,	,, ,,
3978	Pte.	ALLEN, F. W.	,,	,, ,,
3760	,,	BUSBY, E. W.	,,	,, ,,
5331	,,	CRAWFORD, F. K.	,,	,, ,,
5544	,,	BUGGS, E. W.	3/5/17	Killed in Action
2988	,,	BREN, J. F.	,,	,, ,,
4074	,,	BUSHNIE, D. L.	,,	,, ,,
4077	L.-Cpl.	CLEARY, L. J.	,,	,, ,,
3788	Pte.	CULMSEE, R. J.	,,	,, ,,
4414	,,	DILLEY, W.	,,	,, ,,
3798	,,	CHATLEY, N. C.	,,	,, ,,
3826	,,	DONEY, H. S.	,,	,, ,,
2118	,,	FOX, E. F.	22-28/7/16	,, ,,
4231	,,	WOODWORD, A. W.	21/5/17	Died of Wounds
5109	,,	WILSON, J.	25/5/17	,, ,,
431	,,	MORRISON, C.	3/5/17	Killed in Action
5573	,,	DUNLOP, W.	11/5/17	Died of Wounds
	Capt.	HOGARTH, E. G.	3/5/17	Killed in Action
5058	Pte.	MILLS, W.	2/6/17	Died of Wounds
5072	,,	PAGE, C.	1/6/17	Died of Wounds
6172	,,	WILLIAMS, B.	3/5/17	Killed in Action
6902	,,	SHARP, D.	1/7/17	Died of Wounds
5020	,,	GUNN, D. D.	3/5/17	Killed in Action
	2nd Lieut.	MASSIE, H. V.	8/3/17	Died, Pris. of War
5073	Pte.	PEACOCK, W. A.	26/2/17	,, ,,
679	,,	REED, A. T.	5/8/16	Killed in Action

ROLL OF HONOUR

No.	Rank.	Name.	Date of Death.	Cause of Death.
269	Pte.	WALL, B.	5/8/16	Killed in Action
	2nd Lieut.	YEADON, C. F. (M.C.)	”	” ”
2435	Pte.	TURNER, G. (correct name, HALM, L. A.)	”	” ”
3944	”	SMITH, J. H.	”	” ”
1887	”	BETTLES, C. L.	29/7/16	” ”
3925	”	SHECK, G.	5/8/16	” ”
2321	”	WARNER, A. E.	”	” ”
221	”	NICKSON, F.	25/2/17	” ”
546	”	AUBREY, F. V.	5/8/16	” ”
1185	”	COUSINS, P.	”	” ”
5307	”	ADAMSON, A. T.	3/5/17	” ”
	Lieut.	GREIG, G. O.	17/9/17	Killed in Action
5030	Pte.	HILTON, F.	20/9/17	Died of Wounds
5656	”	PATTINSON, A. J.	18/9/17	” ”
1564	”	SAXON, J. S.	4/8/16	Killed in Action
2233	”	TAYLOR, J.	5/8/16	” ”
6161	”	TRITTON, W. G. L.	19/9/17	Died of Wounds
6188	”	WILSON, S.	17/9/17	Killed in Action
6060	”	COLEMAN, F. A.	18/9/17	” ”
6141	”	REID, C.	17/9/17	Died of Wounds
6048	”	BAKER, R. H.	18/9/17	Killed in Action
5141	”	MITCHELL, J. J.	”	” ”
6427	”	PENNY, W.	22-23/9/17	” ”
4552	”	ST. LEON, A. E.	”	” ”
63	”	WRIGHT, H. E.	”	” ”
2041	”	ROBERTSON, D. H.	”	” ”
5796	”	FRASER, T.	23/9/17	” ”
1969	”	TOPEN, J.	17/9/17	” ”
6343	”	GREWAR, A.	16/9/17	” ”
6440	”	HUDSON, J. S.	16/9/17	” ”
5061	Cpl.	MORRISON, H. A.	16/9/17	” ”
1200	T.-Cpl.	WETZEL, H. C.	17/9/17	” ”
6306	Pte.	CRAIG, D. V.	”	” ”
6291	”	BENNETT, A. J.	20/9/17	Died of Wounds
713	”	WILSON, A. M.	”	Killed in Action
3799	”	CHAPPELL, C. C.	”	” ”
3891	”	McEWAN, J. A.	16/9/17	” ”
5370	”	HOLROYD, J. T.	16/9/17	Died of Wounds
6416	”	OGDEN, A.	18/9/17	” ”
756	”	MacDONALD, A. D.	”	” ”
4737	Sgt.	KELLY, V. W.	”	Killed in Action
1547	Pte.	GRIEVE, J. A.	”	” ”
5955	”	NICHOL, W. D.	16/9/17	” ”
306	Cpl.	GAY, T.	21-22/9/17	” ”
540	Pte.	RAY, M. W.	18/9/17	” ”
295	Sgt.	BAILES, J. C.	21-22/9/17	” ”
5343	Pte.	EDWARDS, S. G.	”	” ”
6453	”	ROBINSON, G. W.	”	” ”
6420	”	PRIDHAM, F. D.	”	” ”
2138	L.-Cpl.	EGAN, A.	25/9/17	Died of Wounds
4999	Pte.	COWELL, F. A.	23/9/17	” ”
	2nd Lieut.	McINTYRE, J. A.	4/10/17	Killed in Action
4491	Pte.	MERRITT, F. T.	3/5/17	” ”
4711	”	GLASS, H.	4/10/17	Died of Wounds
1917	Cpl.	JAMES, W. M.	”	” ”

ROLL OF HONOUR

No.	Rank.	Name.	Date of Death.	Cause of Death.
2277	Pte.	FISHER, A.	8/10/17	Died of Wounds
3883	"	McGRATH, C. A.		Killed in Action
	Lieut.	SKENE-SMITH, A. (M.C.)	9/10/17	" "
5838	Pte.	BUCHANAN, G. A.	6/10/17	Died of Wounds
4719	"	HAMILTON, H.	8/10/17	" "
3926	"	SLADE, H.	10/10/17	" "
5700	"	WEST, W. D.	8/10/17	" "
6453	"	HALLIDAY, W. H.	4/10/17	" "
4432	"	FORDEN, A. E.	6/10/17	" "
5981	"	LOWMAN, L. J. T.	5/10/17	" "
4434	L.-Cpl.	FRASER, J.	16/9/17	Killed in Action
4986	Pte.	BRAGG, J. G.	18/9/17	" "
1803	"	McQUALTER, D. R.	11/10/17	" "
6063	"	COX, J. C.	18/9/17	" "
6089	"	GRANT, D. A.	22/9/17	" "
6288	"	BEVERIDGE, G. R.	11/10/17	Died of Wounds
3577	"	LARKIN, M. W.	20/10/17	" "
6135	"	PRIOR, A. J.	3/5/17	Killed in Action
4496	"	MOONEY, J. P.	"	" "
5712	"	GRADY, W. H.	4/10/17	" "
5886	"	HASSETT, J. M.	3/5/17	" "
6170	"	WALLIS, B. T.	3/5/17	Killed in Action
1109	L.-Cpl.	MARTIN, C.	3/5/17	" "
6111	Pte.	LOMAX, C. M.	4/10/17	" "
6099	"	HAWKEN, T. L.	"	" "
6153	"	STEPHENS, W. B.	"	" "
5044	"	LAWLOR, R. B.	"	" "
5054	"	MAXWELL, E. A.	3/10/17	" "
3910	"	RHODES, J. A.	"	" "
5059	"	MINTON, E. A.	"	" "
5430	"	WATSON, H. T.	"	" "
6280	"	BETHUNE, A. T.	4/10/17	" "
1179	"	BRIMSLOW, W.	"	" "
3807	"	COX, O. G.	"	" "
4686	Sgt.	CORDER, R.	"	" "
950	Pte.	COLE, F. H.	"	" "
584	Sgt.	CRANER, A. E.	"	" "
5443	Pte.	CRAWFORD, J.	"	" "
6319	"	DOBSON, T.	"	" "
1895	"	EVANS, A. W.	"	" "
163	"	GRIGSBY, A.	"	" "
5016	"	GORDON, T.	"	" "
5363	"	HANNAKER, J.	"	" "
408	Sgt.	JOHNSON, W.	"	" "
509	"	JONES, H. R. H.	"	" "
5041	Pte.	KELLY, T. A.	"	" "
849	"	LEE, E.	"	" "
5636	"	MAYS, C. W.	"	" "
5404	"	McCARTHY, D. C.	"	" "
5631	"	MOORE, H. G.	"	" "
6415	"	OSBORNE, W. G.	"	" "
2500	"	PARRY, C. H.	"	" "
4775	"	PETERSON, D. G. W.	"	" "
6434	"	STAFFORD, J. G.	"	" "
2371	"	SYMONS, E.	"	" "
928	"	TOWNSEND, W.	"	" "

ROLL OF HONOUR

No.	Rank.	Name.	Date of Death.	Cause of Death.
3957	Pte.	WALKERDEN, R.	4/10/17	Killed in Action
5694	,,	WILSON, W. V.	,,	,, ,,
6448	,,	YOUNG, S.	,,	,, ,,
4978	,,	BATES, W. H.	5/10/17	,, ,,
6362	,,	HUTCHINSON, E. A.	,,	,, ,,
4736	,,	JOHNSON, J. W.	,,	,, ,,
3880	,,	MIDDLEMAS, R.	,,	,, ,,
6396	,,	MONTEFIORE, T.	,,	,, ,,
4196	Cpl.	RALSTON, W. N.	,,	,, ,,
5689	Pte.	THOMPSON, A. V.	,,	,, ,,
1542	,,	BLOM, R. C.	4/10/17	,, ,,
661	,,	PEKIN, J.	,,	,, ,,
6162	,,	TAYLOR, H. J.	9/10/17	,, ,,
5411	,,	SCOTT, S. A.	8/10/17	,, ,,
4652	,,	ANDREW, S.	9/10/17	,, ,,
4976	,,	AUSTIN, G. L.	,,	,, ,,
4989	,,	BRIGGS, D. R.	,,	,, ,,
5323	,,	CAMPBELL, D.	,,	,, ,,
4092	,,	DECKER, A.	,,	,, ,,
4712	,,	GIRVAN, J.	,,	,, ,,
5095	,,	SUTCLIFFE, H.	,,	,, ,,
6391	,,	MARRIOTT, D.	8/10/17	,, ,,
5953	,,	MITCHELL, W. E.	9/10/17	,, ,,
6384	,,	LEES, V. J.	10/10/17	,, ,,
1926	L.-Sgt.	LOWERY, J. J.	2/10/17	,, ,,
4417	Pte.	DRAPER, R. E.	,,	,, ,,
2258	,,	BROWN, S. G.	3/10/17	,, ,,
6435	,,	SMITH, J. R.	2/10/17	,, ,,
5658	,,	PAGE, L. R.	,,	,, ,,
6338	,,	FRY, J.	3/10/17	,, ,,
6333	,,	ELLIOTT, L. D. F.	,,	,, ,,
5963	Sgt.	DALTON, W.	3/10/17	Killed in Action
4448	Pte.	GREEN, W. H.	,,	,, ,,
5970	,,	HEDLEY, F. J.	,,	,, ,,
5029	,,	HILL, A. G.	,,	,, ,,
6367	,,	JEFFREYS, L. G.	,,	,, ,,
399a	,,	DAVIDSON, G. E.	,,	,, ,,
	Lieut.	BLANCHARD, R.	4/10/17	,, ,,
5138	Pte.	McEWAN, W. E.	3/10/17	,, ,,
5889	,,	HOGAN, J. S.	4/10/17	,, ,,
384b	,,	WALLETT, R. E.	3/11/17	,, ,,
5478	,,	SMITH, D. R.	3/10/17	,, ,,
2246	Sgt.	MARSHALL, T.	9/11/17	Died of Wounds
285	Pte.	WILLIAMS, P.	3/10/17	Killed in Action
897	,,	SCOTT, G. A.	9/12/17	Illness
5010	,,	GALBRAITH, W. R.	24/11/17	Died of Wounds
3981	,,	KIRKMAN, J. R.	5/10/17	Killed in Action
1224	L.-Cpl.	BLONDETT, A. J.	11/11/17	,, ,,
4544	Pte.	STURGESS, A.	5/12/17	Died of Wounds
5946	,,	HILLS, F. T.	4/10/17	Killed in Action
6429	,,	ROWE, A. J.	,,	,, ,,
6132	,,	PENN, L.	3/5/17	,, ,,
1182	,,	WHITECROSS, R. H.	3/1/18	Died of Wounds
1090	,,	TWIST, C. J.	18/9/17	Killed in Action
655	L.-Cpl.	NORTHCOTT, C. L.	,,	,, ,,
5043	Pte.	KUNIN, G.	,,	,, ,,

ROLL OF HONOUR

No.	Rank.	Name.	Date of Death.	Cause of Death.
5566	Pte.	CAREY, C. H.	18/9/17	Killed in Action
1927	L.-Cpl.	MATHER, C. G.	4/10/17	,, ,,
6056	Pte.	CHRISTEY, J. W.	3/5/17	,, ,,
6113	,,	LEWIS, C. T.	,,	,, ,,
6116	,,	LANDERS, H. D. M.	,,	,, ,,
6092	,,	HEADY, J.	,,	,, ,,
6164	,,	UNDERWOOD, J. T.	,,	,, ,,
6029	,,	ANDERSON, G. V.	,,	,, ,,
929	,,	UNDERWOOD, L.	,,	,, ,,
5608	,,	HARRINGTON, H. W.	3/5/17	,, ,,
5931	L.-Cpl.	HURLEY, J. C.	,,	,, ,,
5001	Pte.	DAVIDSON, W. S.	,,	,, ,,
4120	,,	HILL, G. J.	,,	,, ,,
5885	,,	GRIFFITHS, H. W.	,,	,, ,,
2614	,,	HOWAT, G. A.	,,	,, ,,
5576	,,	DAVIES, A. E.	,,	,, ,,
5330	,,	CRANE, E. P. W.	,,	,, ,,
5880	,,	COWELL, C. A. N.	,,	,, ,,
4395	,,	COLLINS, D.	,,	,, ,,
5447	,,	CAUDRY, W. J.	,,	,, ,,
5651	,,	OLSEN, H. V.	,,	,, ,,
3893	,,	NOAKE, A.	,,	,, ,,
216	,,	MURRAY, T. J.	,,	,, ,,
2000	,,	MORTON, J. T.	,,	,, ,,
2728	,,	MORRISON, W. B.	,,	,, ,,
5971	,,	BATT, H. L.	,,	,, ,,
3877	,,	MOON, W.	5/8/16	,, ,,
5554	,,	BAILEY, F. E.	3/5/17	,, ,,
5537	Cpl.	ANDREW, P. C.	,,	,, ,,
2433	Pte.	TAYLOR, L. J.	5/8/16	,, ,,
2228	,,	STEVENS, W. J.	,,	,, ,,
1958	L.-Cpl.	SMART, R. J.	5/8/16	,, ,,
5822	Pte.	SMITH, A.	3/5/17	,, ,,
5091	,,	SHANKS, G. C. R.	,,	,, ,,
2410	,,	SCOTT, P. N.	,,	,, ,,
3245	L.-Cpl.	SCHULZE, H.	,,	,, ,,
3230	,,	ROBINSON, S.	,,	,, ,,
4194	,,	RENSHAW, H.	,,	,, ,,
4778	Pte	PRITCHARD, W. R.	,,	,, ,,
3901	,,	PRICE, H.	,,	,, ,,
2769	,,	PHILLIPS, W. M.	,,	,, ,,
5654	,,	PETERSEN, C. M. H.	,,	,, ,,
5901	,,	PARKER, J. McD.	3/5/17	,, ,,
661	,,	OWEN, T. H.	,,	,, ,,
1155	,,	KING, E. J.	5/8/16	,, ,,
593	,,	ELLIS, F.	,,	,, ,,
1948	,,	ROSS, F. C.	27/7/16	,, ,,
1171	,,	O'CONNELL, W.	,,	,, ,,
5962	,,	WOODS, A.	3/5/17	,, ,,
4569	,,	WINSOR, A.	,,	,, ,,
493	,,	WIEDMANN, O. B.	,,	,, ,,
4801	,,	WEST, J.	,,	,, ,,
5305	,,	TREGONING, W. J.	,,	,, ,,
3941	L.-Cpl.	SWIFT, R.	,,	,, ,,
3924	,,	SWANEY, V.	,,	,, ,,
1108	Sgt.	SUTTON, E.	,,	,, ,,

ROLL OF HONOUR

No.	Rank.	Name.	Date of Death.	Cause of Death.
4192	Pte.	RIXON, A. J.	5/8/16	Killed in Action
6276	”	ANSON, A. G.	4/10/17	” ”
5716	”	CATTON, J. T.	3/5/17	” ”
130	”	CAMPBELL, W. C.	”	” ”
4369	”	BLOORE, A. E. G.	”	” ”
5372	”	JOHNSON, J. W.	”	” ”
5597	”	HUNT, L. C. A.	”	” ”
4974	”	AMERY, A. S.	”	” ”
4059	”	ARMSTRONG, P.	”	” ”
4985	”	BOWYER, H.	”	” ”
4977	”	BARKER, W. H.	”	” ”
5787	”	BERLOWITZ, J. T.	2/5/17	” ”
5632	”	MITCHELL, J. L.	3/5/17	” ”
416	”	KINSEY, H. L.	”	” ”
4742	”	LOWE, H.	”	” ”
5379	L.-Cpl.	MADDEN, W. C.	”	” ”
4492	Pte.	MILLER, C.	”	” ”
5580	”	ELLIOTT, P. N.	”	” ”
4431	”	FOLEY, F. J.	3/5/17	” ”
155	”	GASCOYNE, A.	2/5/17	” ”
2033	”	DENNETT, C. H.	”	” ”
5781	”	DUNKLEY, C. B.	3/5/17	” ”
5296	Cpl.	HUGHES, R. E.	”	” ”
3952	Pte.	TAYLOR, W. C.	”	” ”
5718	”	SOMERS, M. D.	”	” ”
5406	”	ROBIE, A. D.	”	” ”
5906	”	RICKARD, E. M.	”	” ”
1724	Cpl.	PETERSON, J. R.	”	” ”
5067	Pte.	McPHERSON, D.	”	” ”
5049	”	LOVELL, H. (Alias Dowell, D. R.)	”	” ”
4728	L.-Cpl.	JOHANSEN, H. P. B.	”	” ”
1026	”	FORSTER, C. E.	”	” ”
2177a	Pte.	DAVIS, O. V.	”	” ”
4404	”	CRUMP, C. T. W.	”	” ”
4683	”	CRAWFORD, J.	”	” ”
4383	”	BROWNING, W. A.	”	” ”
4375	”	BOSUSTOW, W. J.	”	” ”
1691	L.-Cpl.	CAMPBELL, W.	5/8/16	” ”
4384	Pte.	BURKE, W. J.	”	” ”
2014	”	BROWN, E. T. E.	”	” ”
1666	T.-Sgt.	BRADLEY, A. W.	”	” ”
2572a	Pte.	BODINNAR, W. T.	”	” ”
464	”	SMYTHE, R.	”	” ”
1087	Sgt.	SHIELDS, J. H.	”	” ”
2415	Pte.	SHAW, A. H.	”	” ”
448	Cpl.	REID, J.	”	” ”
2355	Pte.	QUINN, J. F.	”	” ”
747	”	PRICE, D. R.	”	” ”
3209	T.-Cpl.	O'HALLORAN, J. E.	”	” ”
1213	Pte.	BROWN, H.	”	” ”
243	”	SHARP, C. H.	”	” ”
4585	”	COLEMAN, H.	5/8/16	” ”
2124	”	WHITE, F.	”	” ”
1785	”	STRAKER, P.	”	” ”
4136	”	HADFIELD, A.	”	” ”

ROLL OF HONOUR

No.	Rank.	Name.	Date of Death.	Cause of Death.
1914	Pte	INSEAL, A. G.	5/8/16	Killed in Action
1430	Sgt.	TAYLOR, D. E.	”	” ”
1814	Pte.	NORMAN, H. A.	”	” ”
189	”	LEWIS, A. E.	”	” ”
4129	”	HORROCKS, C. H. J.	”	” ”
4134	”	HANCOCK, H. E.	”	” ”
4110	”	GOSS, A. I.	”	” ”
1713	”	FELL, V. H.	”	” ”
140	T.-Cpl.	DAVIDSON, P. J.	”	” ”
471	Pte.	SYMMONS, M. R.	”	” ”
324	”	ALLEN, J. N.	”	” ”
3962	”	WILSON, W. S.	4/8/16	” ”
1787	”	THOMPSON, A. H.	”	” ”
487	L.-Cpl.	WATSON, A. A.	”	” ”
3779	Pte.	BARDIOUX, F. E.	26/8/16	” ”
765	”	WHITE, S. R.	”	” ”
2852	”	HOLMES, F. J.	”	” ”
3897	”	NEIL, J.	”	” ”
2019	”	BUTLER, A.	”	” ”
3639	”	SMITH, L.	”	” ”
1889	”	CALLANDER, N.	25/2/17	” ”
	Lieut.	FRASER, H. P.	3/5/17	” ”
3961	Pte.	WILKINS, L. W.	5/8/16	” ”
1190	”	SWIRE, A.	4/8/16	” ”
701	Sgt.	TREVENA, T. S.	5/8/16	” ”
6039	Pte.	BRYANT, H. E.	14/10/17	” ”
705a	”	KENNEDY, M. F.	18/9/17	” ”
4572	”	YOUNG, F. L.	4/10/17	” ”
3974	”	WALKER, A.	16/1/16	” ”
4770	”	McKENZIE, J. A.	4/10/17	” ”
1948	”	ROSS, F. C.	”	” ”
5088	”	ROWE, F.	4/10/17	” ”
6775	”	CORIDAS, L. J.	9/3/18	” ”
1941	”	O'LEARY, E.	”	” ”
5649	”	O'REILLY, J. A.	”	” ”
	2nd Lieut.	ROBBINS, C. A. L.	10/3/18	” ”
907	Pte.	STEVENSON, R.	27/7/16	” ”
	2nd Lieut.	PARSONS, W. H. (M.M., C. de G.)	26/3/18	Died of Wounds
5148	Pte.	SIMMONDS, E. G.	27/3/18	” ”
3814	L.-Cpl.	DAMON, G. L.	11/4/18	” ”
1121	Pte.	BOYCE, G. H.	13/4/18	Killed in Action
2457	”	YULE, R. O.	14/4/18	” ”
5312	”	BARTLETT, T. N.	27/3/18	” ”
4765a	”	CAMPBELL, W.	10/4/18	” ”
664	”	O'NEILL, A.	26/3/18	” ”
6851	”	MITCHELL, F. J.	27/3/18	Injuries (Accid.)
5060	”	MORAN, P. F.	10/4/18	Died of Wounds
1925	”	LEE, J. S.	3/4/18	Killed in Action
4104	”	FOOTS, J. M.	22/4/18	” ”
549	Sgt.	ASPINALL, R.	15/4/18	” ”
4400	”	CORRY, V. C.	18/4/18	” ”
4675	Pte.	COLHOUN, G. E.	24/4/18	” ”
807	”	DERMONDY, P. G.	23/4/18	” ”
5876	”	DOUGLAS, O. H.	24/4/18	” ”
6918	”	WADE, T. A.	10/5/18	Died of Wounds

ROLL OF HONOUR

No.	Rank.	Name.	Date of Death.	Cause of Death.
6180	Pte	BRIDGES, R. G.	4/10/17	Killed in Action
6062	"	COBDEN, R.	3/5/17	" "
6137	"	PERRY, J. F. A.	9/10/17	" "
3775	L.-Cpl.	BELL, C.	3/10/17	" "
	2nd Lieut.	BOWDEN, C. M.	19/5/18	" "
4690	Pte.	COBBAN, WM.	4/10/17	" "
5611	L.-Cpl.	HOAR, C. H.	"	" "
5700	Pte.	JOHNS, J. A.	4/10/17	Killed in Action
622	"	LOCKWOOD, F. H.	15/5/18	" "
3865	"	LYNCH, P.	9/10/17	" "
1580	"	MULLIGAN, C. L.	4/10/17	" "
5301	"	McCOWAN, N.	3/5/17	" "
4178	"	NORTHEY, F. H.	"	" "
4423	L.-Cpl.	SALAN, E. C.	4/10/17	" "
2378	Pte.	SCOTT, J. D.	9/10/17	" "
5684	"	SMITH, R. F.	25/2/17	" "
5792	Cpl.	DAVIS, A. W.	21/5/18	Died of Wounds
2709	Pte.	LAWRENCE, J. C.	"	" "
4021	"	McDEVITT, H.	22/5/18	" "
6896a	"	SNOW, H. A.	19/5/18	" "
1187a	L.-Cpl.	TOURRIOR, W. A. (M.M.)	9/10/17	" "
1617	Cpl.	STORR, J. L.	25/5/18	" "
6031	Pte.	ARROW, D. P.	14/5/18	Killed in Action
6094	"	GARD, E. P.	19/5/18	" "
5538	"	ALLOWAY, A.	"	" "
6768a	"	AMES, B.	20/5/18	" "
67801	"	CLARK, W. L.	19/5/18	" "
6938	"	CROWLEY, D.	18/5/18	" "
5937	"	CURNICK, L. V.	19/5/18	" "
6789a	"	DAVIDSON, G. A.	"	" "
6798	"	FRASER, J. L.	"	" "
3833	"	GOSDEN, J. M.	"	" "
4482	"	LOCKWOOD, A.	"	" "
6379	"	LORRIGAN, W. F.	14/5/18	" "
6862	"	McKENZIE, P.	19/5/18	" "
4501	"	MULHOLLAND, E. S.	"	" "
4761	"	MURPHY, W. A.	"	" "
5084	"	RIZZO, THOS.	"	" "
6436	"	SMEATON, J. L.	"	" "
6895a	"	SMEETON, J. E.	"	" "
6900	"	STAFF, C. R.	19/5/18	Killed in Action
2386	"	STUCKEY, E. N.	"	" "
6996	"	THOMAS, A. C.	"	" "
5691	"	WILTON, C. T. (M.M.)	"	" "
736	"	BARTON, W. G.	"	Died of Wounds
6809	"	FRASER, W.	"	" "
760a	"	HARRISON, F. L.	"	" "
766	"	ROBERTSON, C. C.	"	" "
6876	"	PETHER, F. T.	12/5/18	Killed in Action
5893	"	RIDDELL, A. H.	30/5/18	Died of Wounds
2672	"	ATKINS, W.	14/5/18	Killed in Action
6799	"	DURHAM, W. J.	19/5/18	" "
	Lieut.	LENNON, J.	9/6/18	" "
6838	Pte.	McCARTHY, M. J.	14/6/18	Died of Wounds
5943	"	GRAHAM, J. B.	13/6/18	" "
2278	Dvr.	GREEN, P. J.	9/6/18	" "

ROLL OF HONOUR

No.	Rank.	Name.	Date of Death.	Cause of Death.
4805	Pte.	WATTS, A.	9/6/18	Killed in Action
750	Sgt.	SMITH, E. A.	7/6/18	,, ,,
6904	T.-Sgt.	TYLER, R. J.	9/6/18	,, ,,
6947a	Pte.	ROGAN, L. C.	11/6/18	,, ,,
	Lieut.	KELLEWAY, F. G. (M.C.)	4/10/17	,, ,,
6846	Pte.	LAWSON, A.	30/6/18	Illness (Wounds)
5424	,,	TURTON, W.	15/6/18	Killed in Action
5112	,,	WOOF, R.	6/7/18	,, ,,
	Lieut.	SWANTON, R.	23/7/18	,, ,,
6787a	Pte.	DAHLITZ, E. B.	21/7/18	Died of Wounds
4131	Sgt.	HARRIS, W. C. (D.C.M.)	22/7/18	,, ,,
2191	Pte.	LUKE, J.	21/7/18	,, ,,
6892a	,,	SIGG, G. H.	23/7/18	,, ,,
2381	,,	SMILLIE, A.	22/7/18	,, ,,
5118	,,	BYRNE, G. A.	,,	Killed in Action
681	,,	RUSSELL, L.	27/7/18	Illness (Wounds)
6920a	,,	WINTER, L.	23/7/18	Killed in Action
754a	,,	DEANE, W.	3/8/18	Died of Wounds
391	,,	HALLYBURTON, A. B.	27/7/18	Killed in Action
6942	,,	SHEARGOLD, E. F.	,,	,, ,,
6856	,,	MADDEN, W. G.	,,	,, ,,
6369	Pte.	JOSE, J. J.	24/7/18	,, ,,
5917	,,	THORNELL, E. A.	9/8/18	Illness
283	Cpl.	WIGGER, R. B.	5/8/18	Died of Wounds
	Lieut.	MADDEN, N. J. (M.C.)	18/8/18	Killed in Action
		McCARTIN, L. A. (M.C.)		
2234	Pte.	THOMPSON, T. H.	17/8/18	Died of Wounds
3829	Sgt.	FOURACRE, R. S.	14/8/18	Killed in Action
6910	Pte.	THOMAS, H.	13/8/18	,, ,,
773	,,	ANDERSON, G. J.	18/8/18	,, ,,
873		NORRIS, J.	,,	,, ,,
	Lieut.	WALL, H. M. M. (M.C.)	27/8/18	,, ,,
6894a	Pte.	SMITH, E. W.	18/8/18	Died of Wounds
1049	Cpl.	BAILLIE, R. G.	1/9/18	
123	Sgt.	BREGENZER, E. R. (D.C.M.)	18/8/18	Killed in Action
4002		ELLIS, L. G.	,,	,, ,,
6079	Pte.	COFFEY, S.	27/8/18	,, ,,
3791	Cpl.	COATES, F. H.	,,	,, ,,
5117	Pte.	LAYBURN, W. J. A. (M.M.)	28/8/18	,, ,,
233	Cpl.	RASDELL, F. L.	27/8/18	,, ,,
1086	,,	SPARGO, H. J.	28/8/18	,, ,,
6310	,,	CORNELL, E.	2/9/18	Died of Wounds
5681	,,	SARGEANT, H.	3/9/18	,, ,,
3836	,,	GILL, H.	27/8/18	Killed in Action
6364	,,	HURST, H.	9/10/17	,, ,,
50128	,,	POWELL, W. H.	28/8/18	,, ,,
5016	,,	WILLIAMSON, L. A.	9/9/18	Died of Wounds
50029	,,	CUNNINGHAM, L. N.	2/9/18	Killed in Action
6332	,,	EDWARDS, R. G. C.	,,	,, ,,
6350	,,	HENDERSON, T. C.	,,	,, ,,
50075	,,	JONES, W. S.	,,	,, ,,
4510	,,	NANKERVIS, W. C.	,,	,, ,,
5918	,,	TREMBATH, H. E.	1/9/18	
5419	,,	TOMKINSON, J. H.	6/10/18	Died of Wounds
	Lieut.	PATERSON, E. E. (M.C.)	3/10/18	Killed in Action

ROLL OF HONOUR

No.	Rank.	Name.	Date of Death.	Cause of Death.
2012	Pte.	WHITE, A. T.	10/10/18	Died of Wounds
4653	"	ADAMS, E. H.	3/10/18	Killed in Action
	Capt.	BRAITHWAITE, W. McC. (M.C.)	"	" "
4747	Pte.	LAURENCE, R.	"	" "
1936	"	McALPINE, A.	"	" "
1577	"	MITCHELL, J. E. P.	"	" "
51453	"	STEVENS, E. H.	4/10/18	" "
4699	"	ELLISON, J.	5/10/18	" "
6808	"	GANE, C.	3/10/18	" "
51455	"	SUGDEN, J.	"	" "
6948	"	TUCKER, S. W.	"	" "
4374	Cpl.	BONNETT, R. P.	9/6/18	" "
6290	Pte.	BUNWORTH, D. F.	4/10/18	" "
6788a	"	DAVEY, T. H. W.	"	" "
3823	"	DAVIS, A.	"	" "
	2nd Lieut.	DAWSETT, P. J.	"	" "
6812a	Pte.	GLEESON, W. J.	"	" "
3984	"	GOGOLL, C. H.	"	" "
4116	"	GRAHAM, F. W.	"	" "
678a	"	KELLEY, P. L.	"	" "
50091	"	LEGGE, G. F.	"	" "
5625	L.-Sgt.	LIGHT, E.	"	" "
6401	Cpl.	McCALL, J. P. (M.M.)	"	" "
50194	Pte.	POOLE, C. E.	"	" "
5078	"	POULTER, J. W.	"	" "
2409	L.-Cpl.	SPARKS, H. T.	3/10/18	" "
5102	Pte.	WALKERDEN, A.	4/10/18	" "
6287	"	BRAIN, J.	"	" "
51410	"	McLENNAN, M. W.	"	" "
51372	"	HENDRICK, R. R.	"	" "
6857	"	MAXWELL, W.	18/8/18	" "
3904	"	PODMORE, J.	1/11/18	Illness
6796	"	DOWLING, O. W. L.	8/12/18	"
4774a	L.-Cpl.	SMITH, P. E. (M.M.)	10/11/18	"
5813	Pte.	McNEIL, D. C.	28/11/18	"
1979	"	MORRIS, A.	18/8/18	Killed in Action
6101	L.-Cpl.	JACKSON, J. D.	"	" "
3825	L.-Sgt.	DOLAN, F.	18/8/18	" "
1071	Pte.	EGAN, H. J.	"	" "
398	Sgt.	HEFFERNAN, J.	"	" "
6360	Pte.	HILL, V. G.	"	" "
6361	"	HURST, A. S.	"	" "
6946	"	KELLY, E. J.	"	" "
	Lieut.	WESTAWAY, H. W.	"	" "
6903	Pte.	WARWICK, W. J.	8/2/19	Illness
518	"	McINTYRE, A. J.	18/8/18	Killed in Action
3942	"	SWIFT, T. G. L.	"	" "
4720	"	HANCOCK, F.	19/5/18	" "
678	Sgt.	ROLFE, G. T.	10/8/18	" "
5974	Pte.	DE GROOT, R. J.	4/10/18	" "
61868	"	HIGGINS, D. C.	"	" "
6885	"	REYMENT, E. J.	"	" "

NOTE.—Fifty-five members of the Battalion were killed or died of wounds while attached to other units. Their names cannot be enrolled here at present, as, up to time of publication, the necessary particulars could not be made available by the Department of Defence.

Wholly set up and printed in Australia by the Specialty Press Pty. Ltd., 174 Little Collins St., Melbourne

Battalion Headquarters' Company, June, 1918.

"A" Company, June, 1918.

"B" Company, June, 1918.

"C" Company, June, 1918.

"D" Company, June, 1918.

Transport Section, June, 1918.

Part of Nucleus Company, June, 1918.

Part of Nucleus Company, June, 1918.

www.ingramcontent.com/pod-product-compliance
Lightning Source LLC
Chambersburg PA
CBHW080401170426
43193CB00016B/2782